love y̶ library

Buckinghamshire Libraries

Search, renew or reserve online 24/7
www.buckscc.gov.uk/libraries

24 hour renewal line
0303 123 0035

Enquiries
01296 382415

follow us **twitter**

@Bucks_Libraries

INSIGHT ⊙ GUIDES

CAPE TOWN
POCKET GUIDE

95100000242575

PLAN & BOOK
YOUR TAILOR-MADE TRIP

BRAZIL **CHILE** **ECUADOR**

TAILOR-MADE TRIPS & UNIQUE EXPERIENCES CREATED BY LOCAL TRAVEL EXPERTS AT INSIGHTGUIDES.COM/HOLIDAYS

Insight Guides has been inspiring travellers with high-quality travel content for over 45 years. As well as our popular guidebooks, we now offer the opportunity to book tailor-made private trips completely personalised to your needs and interests. By connecting with one of our local experts, you will directly benefit from their expertise and local know-how, helping you create memories that will last a lifetime.

HOW INSIGHTGUIDES.COM/HOLIDAYS WORKS

STEP 1

Pick your dream destination and submit an enquiry, or modify an existing itinerary if you prefer.

STEP 2

Fill in a short form, sharing details of your travel plans and preferences with a local expert.

STEP 3

Your local expert will create your personalised itinerary, which you can amend until you are completely satisfied.

STEP 4

Book securely online. Pack your bags and enjoy your holiday! Your local expert will be available to answer questions during your trip.

BENEFITS OF PLANNING & BOOKING AT INSIGHTGUIDES.COM/HOLIDAYS

PLANNED BY LOCAL EXPERTS

The Insight Guides local experts are hand-picked, based on their experience in the travel industry and their impeccable standards of customer service.

SAVE TIME & MONEY

When a local expert plans your trip, you save time and money when you book, even during high season. You won't be charged for using a credit card either.

TAILOR-MADE TRIPS

Book with Insight Guides, and you will be in complete control of the planning process, from the initial selections to amending your final itinerary.

BOOK & TRAVEL STRESS-FREE

Enjoy stress-free travel when you use the Insight Guides secure online booking platform. All bookings come with a money-back guarantee.

WHAT OTHER TRAVELLERS THINK ABOUT TRIPS BOOKED AT INSIGHTGUIDES.COM/HOLIDAYS

Trip to Vietnam

The organization was superb, the drivers professional, and accommodation quite comfortable. I was well taken care of! My thanks to your colleagues who helped make my trip to Vietnam such a great experience. My only regret is that I couldn't spend more time in the country.

Heather ★★★★★

TOP 10 ATTRACTIONS

LONG STREET
Central Cape Town's liveliest thoroughfare. See page 31.

BOULDERS BEACH
See thousands of African penguins. See page 58.

TABLE MOUNTAIN
This landmark offers sweeping views in all directions. See page 40.

VICTORIA AND ALFRED WATERFRONT
A popular shopping and dining destination. See page 37.

CASTLE OF GOOD HOPE

South Africa's oldest building, dating to 1666. See page 27.

HERMANUS

Go whale-watching. See page 66.

CAPE OF GOOD HOPE NATURE RESERVE

Southern tip of the Cape Peninsula. See page 57.

CAPE WINELANDS

Acres of green vines surround elegant Cape Dutch mansions. See page 63.

KIRSTENBOSCH NATIONAL BOTANICAL GARDEN

Home to beautiful proteas, cycads and the Tree Canopy Walkway. See page 44.

ROBBEN ISLAND

Where Nelson Mandela was held. See page 50.

A PERFECT DAY

9.00am

Good Coffee; Great People Watching

Start your day with a flat white and croissant at Tamboers Winkel (www.facebook.com/Tamboerswinkel) on the corner of Kloof and De Lorentz Streets, a hip neighbourhood caffeine den on the side of Table Mountain. Enjoy a cup of coffee among bloggers, models and Capetonians alike.

10.00am

Get your Green On

Stroll through the open-air market at Greenmarket Square, where you will find a variety of vendors selling clothing and sandals, as well as African jewellery, art, and fabrics.

12.00pm

The Call to Kalk Bay

Jump on the train south to Kalk Bay, to breathe the fresh sea air as you amble along cobblestone streets past tiny galleries and antique shops. The name Kalk Bay is derived from days when seashells were once baked in kilns along the shoreline to produce lime (kalk in Afrikaans). Buy seafood straight off the boat the fish are still wriggling – or at one of the harbourside cafes. If you're feeling energetic, climb one of th stairways to Boyes Drive, where you can spot whales False Bay below.

11.00am

Art Old and New

Cross the Company's Garden to the South African National Gallery, where you can view a cornucopia of old masters and South African contemporary art; loo out for Jane Alexander's three ghoulish figures, The Butcher Boys (1985–86), a response to the horrors of apartheid. The gallery is representative of South African history – as told through art.

N CAPE TOWN

.00pm

hame and History

ate afternoon, head back to the central V&A Waterfront
catch the last ferry to Robben Island, which leaves at
pm. Tours of the island are led by former prisoners, who
recall hunger strikes and prison life under apartheid. The
rry ride over takes about half hour while the tour itself
sts around three. See this symbol of the apartheid era
948–90) and you will come to understand more about
outh Africa's present and future challenges.

.00pm

ilo and Tapas

epping off the Robben Island ferry at the Nelson
andela Gateway, you are close to the restaurants and
ars of the V&A Waterfront, city centre and Atlantic
uburbs. Perhaps wander through the Waterfront's Silo
istrict, and past the impressive repurposed concrete
lo housing the Zeitz MOCAA (Museum of Contemporary
rt Africa), to pick up a taxi. Tapas is popular in Cape
own, and the city's excellent small-plate restaurants
clude La Parada, which has branches at the Waterfront
nd on Bree Street, and Chef's Warehouse & Canteen,
so on Bree. Especially at the latter, you will be wowed
y one of the most innovative menus in Cape Town,
xcellent service, and a stylish setting. The small tapas
ishes are especially tasty and easy to share.

8.30pm

Culture Fix

Head round the corner
to the Waiting Room
(www.facebook.com/
WaitingRoomCT)
at 273 Long Street,
where live bands and
DJs attract a young
crowd most nights.
For some highbrow
entertainment,
choral and classical
performances take
place at the famous
St. George's Cathedral
(www.sgcathedral.
co.za), and the Cape
Town Philharmonic
Orchestra (www.cpo.
org.za) regularly plays
City Hall. Beneath the
cathedral, the Crypt
Jazz Restaurant (www.
thecryptjazz.com) is an
atmospheric venue for
live jazz from Tuesday
to Saturday.

CONTENTS

⬤ INTRODUCTION _____ 10

🏛 HISTORY _____ 15

📖 WHERE TO GO _____ 27

City Centre _____ 27
Around the Castle of Good Hope 27, Adderley Street 30, Around
Long Street 32, Government Avenue 33, Bo-Kaap 35

Victoria And Alfred Waterfront _____ 37

Table Mountain _____ 40

Southern Suburbs _____ 44
Kirstenbosch National Botanical Garden 44, Constantia 46, Other
Suburbs 48

Robben Island _____ 50

Excursions _____ 56
Cape Peninsula to Cape Point 54, Stellenbosch and the
Winelands 60, Stellenbosch to Franschhoek 64, Hermanus and
the Overberg 66, The Garden Route 71, The West Coast and
Cederberg 79

😊 WHAT TO DO _____ 85

Shopping _____ 85
Entertainment _____ 88
Sports _____ 91
Beaches _____ 95

Children's Cape Town_____98
Scenic Train Journeys_____99

🍵 **EATING OUT**_____102

🗂 **A-Z TRAVEL TIPS**_____117

🏨 **RECOMMENDED HOTELS**_____136

📖 **INDEX**_____143

🎬 **FEATURES**

Ancient Peaks_____14
Nelson Mandela_____23
Historical Landmarks_____25
Cultural Cape Town_____41
Carpets of Flowers_____48
Township Tours_____53
History of Robben Island_____55
Cape Dutch Architecture_____63
Helshoogte Pass_____67
Gentle Giants_____70
Route 62: Top Tip_____77
Lights, Camera, Cape Town!_____79
Feather Millionaires_____83
Guides and Tours_____89
Calendar of Events_____101
Rooibos Tea_____107

INTRODUCTION

From the first sight of the unmistakable profile of Table Mountain, Cape Town works its way into your heart. It is easy to fall in love with the city, and each year millions of people from all over the world do just that. Cosmopolitan Cape Town is one of the leading tourist attractions on the African continent, and two-thirds of all visitors to South Africa include it on their itinerary.

The blend of African, European and Islamic influences that gives the 'Mother City', as South Africa's oldest city is known, its true magic is evident immediately. One minute you feel as if you are standing in 18th-century Holland, gazing up at an elegant, gabled building. The next you are in an African craft market, with splashes of brightly coloured fabrics alongside carved masks. Further on, the narrow, cobbled streets of the Bo-Kaap neighbourhood echo with the sound of the minarets calling the faithful to prayer.

This cultural mix infuses all aspects of Cape Town life. Township jazz rings out from small bars. Galleries exhibit the best of African and European art. A wealth of shops, craft stalls and flea markets sell everything from antiques to African **carvings**, traditional garments to designer clothes, and from gourmet food and local craft beer to fresh fruit and aromatic spices. Cape Town's culinary scene has garnered increasing international attention with fine restaurants offering choices from African cuisine to the distinctive local 'Cape Malay' dishes. People sit at shady sidewalk cafés sipping South African wine and watching street entertainers; expensive yachts dance on the water, mingling with brightly painted fishing boats, sleek cruise liners, and huge container ships laden with cargo from all ports.

POIGNANT PAST

Superb museums chronicle the region's history, stretching beyond the days of the early settlers, European explorers, and even the nomadic hunter-gatherers that first lived there. The exhibits bring to life a history encompassing brutality and bloodshed, including the displacement of the original native peoples, slavery and, during the second half of the 20th century,

Table Mountain

apartheid. There are reminders everywhere: slave lodges in the courtyards of fine mansions; dioramas of ancient peoples whose way of life was overturned by the arrival of the European settlers; and the undeveloped land and poignant museum in District Six (see page 29), a graphic testimony to the divisiveness of apartheid.

A short ferry ride from the V&A Waterfront, Robben Island is now a museum, but more importantly, a symbol of hope. The world remembers it as the prison that held Nelson Mandela, yet its legacy of cruelty extends back more than 300 years. No punches are pulled here; the simple, dignified presentation of the facts is all that is needed to leave visitors reeling. The city has also upped its cultural credentials with the Zeitz MOCAA and Norval Foundation art museums.

Towering above all this activity, rising up like a benevolent giant, is Table Mountain. This legendary landmark first

Girl from Imizamo Yethu township

...beckoned European seafarers here over 500 years ago, and continues to enthral visitors. Wherever you are in the city, it is impossible not to lift your eyes to catch yet another glimpse. Around a million people catch the cable car to the summit each year, to be greeted by magnificent views of the city, the mountains and the ocean, and to walk among the fascinating wildlife and flora on the plateau.

RAINBOW CITY WITH A SUPERB CLIMATE

Perhaps the greatest pleasure gained from visiting Cape Town comes from its inhabitants. Capetonians are laidback and friendly, and everywhere you go you are greeted with a smile. Desmond Tutu famously called South Africa the 'Rainbow Nation', and this sums up the ethnic mix that is Cape Town. The main racial groups are so-called coloured people, black Africans and whites. The term 'coloured' doesn't have the same connotations in South Africa as in Britain and the US, and simply refers to South Africans of mixed race. The coloured population evolved through the intermingling of the earliest inhabitants: the San Bushmen, Khoikhoi herders, descendants of slaves from the East Indies, members of African tribes from the north and east, and European settlers. Other descendants of the slaves retained their Islamic faith, and are today known as the Cape Muslim (or Cape Malay) people. The white population mainly comprises the 'English' of British descent and Afrikaners, whose genealogy includes Dutch, French Huguenot and German blood. Most locals speak English, but the main mother tongues are Afrikaans, spoken by Afrikaners and coloured people, and Xhosa, characterised by its click sounds.

Cape Town is blessed with a Mediterranean climate, and summer (November–March) sees long days of bright sunshine and temperatures approaching 30°C (86°F). There is also much to be said for visiting at other times of the year, not least that you avoid the crowds. One of the city's best-kept secrets is that the Cape is at its most beautiful in autumn (April–May) and spring (September–October). The region's wild flowers are at their spectacular best in spring and whales migrate along the coast during winter and autumn.

SPECTACULAR SETTING

There are mountains everywhere: towering over verdant winelands, cradling picturesque Victorian towns, flanking dense forests, and stretching down towards colourful fishing villages, vast expanses of white-sand beach and sparkling waters teeming with marine life.

Much of this can be explored on day-long excursions from the city. You can follow one of the Wine Routes, around towns such as Stellenbosch and Franschhoek, sampling some of the best South African wines while sitting in a vineyard. Or walk for miles along empty stretches of pristine white sand, spotting whales and dolphins out at sea and decades-old shipwrecks on the beach, then eat delicious seafood in an open-air restaurant set on the shore.

A BRIGHT FUTURE

South Africa is notorious for its history of racial prejudice and segregation, and the legacy of those days can be seen in the Cape Flats, the desolate black townships and coloured areas, where crime and poverty still prevail. However, heartfelt efforts by all sides to come together are also evident. The average Capetonian is appalled by what happened under apartheid and eager to heal the wounds. There is still a great divide between rich and poor, but this is increasingly less along racial lines. Righting the wrongs of the past is a huge undertaking, but the will to succeed is strong.

The local government has made huge efforts to improve security in the city centre. Measures include large numbers of surveillance cameras, mounted police and CCID (Central City Improvement District) officers on patrol. Crime is consequently kept under control in the city centre, and a few basic precautions are all that is needed to have a trouble-free visit – it is important not to visit the townships without a licensed guide (especially at night), for example.

With so much on offer, it is easy to see why so many travellers visit Cape Town and why they find it hard to go home. Chances are, by the time you leave, you'll be planning your next visit.

⊘ ANCIENT PEAKS

The Western Cape's mountains are among the world's oldest, comprising sedimentary mudstones and sandstones laid down 500-plus million years ago. By comparison, the Alps, Andes, Himalayas and Rockies are babies, having emerged within the last 60 million years, while Mounts Kilimanjaro and Kenya, Africa's tallest peaks, are a mere 1 and 3 million years old respectively.

A BRIEF HISTORY

Cape Town has earned many nicknames over the years, but perhaps the most apt is the 'Mother City'. Since the arrival of the first Europeans, it has been the centre for the foundation of modern South Africa.

For tens of thousands of years, this region was the domain of the San Bushmen, nomadic hunter-gathers living off the wealth of game. Beautiful San rock paintings can be seen around the Western Cape, especially in the Cederberg Wilderness Area. The South African Museum in the city centre has some excellent examples preserved in display cases.

Some 2,000 years ago, Khoikhoi cattle herders moved into the area. Although this displaced the San, forcing them inland, the two peoples enjoyed an essentially peaceful coexistence, punctuated by occasional skirmishes. The Khoikhoi tended their herds and traded in cattle with the Bantu-speaking people of the north, and the San continued to hunt antelopes.

THE EXPLORERS ARRIVE

This idyllic life was to change forever in the course of less than 200

Ancient rock carving

Jan van Riebeeck lands in Table Bay

years. In the late 15th century the great European powers were engaged in a race to find the best sea route to India, with tremendous wealth from trade in spices and slaves awaiting those who were successful.

In 1488, in his quest to discover the spice route, Portuguese navigator Bartolomeu Dias was blown off course and unwittingly rounded the Cape of Good Hope in a storm. He continued round Cape Agulhas, which is the southernmost point of Africa, and finally landed at what he named Aguado de São Brás (Watering Place of St Blaize) – present-day Mossel Bay – becoming the first-known European to travel this far south. Today, Mossel Bay marks the start of the famous Garden Route. It houses a marvellous museum commemorating Dias (see page 71), with exhibits including a painstakingly reproduced replica of Dias's original caravel.

Dias originally named his cape the Cape of Storms (Cabo das Tormentas); it was only renamed Cape of Good Hope (Cabo da Boa Esperança) by John II of Portugal after a second Portuguese navigator, Vasco da Gama, succeeded in opening up the route to the East in 1498. The Cape of Good Hope became a vital stopping-off point for ships travelling to the Indies from Europe, with the Khoikhoi soon establishing a thriving trading relationship with the crews. To keep in touch with home during the lengthy voyages, letters were left by sailors under 'post office stones', to be collected by homeward-bound vessels.

The land adjacent to Table Bay was first explored by Europeans in 1503, when yet another Portuguese explorer, Antonio de Saldanha, climbed the great, flat-topped mountain. He named it Table Mountain, carving a cross into the rock at neighbouring Lion's Head which can still be seen.

The link with Europe was to remain largely unobtrusive for 150 years. Ships would call in, stock up and move on. The Cape was renowned for its great beauty – in 1580 Sir Francis Drake wrote that it was 'the fairest cape we saw in the whole circumference of the earth' – but also for the ferocity of the storms which raged off its shores.

COLONISATION BEGINS

In 1652, the Cape of Good Hope fell under the gaze of the mighty Dutch East India Company (Vereenigde Oostindische Compagnie; VOC). Formed by the amalgamation of a number of small trading companies in the early 17th century, the Company had grown in just 50 years to be one of the most powerful organisations on earth, with its own army and fleet. Table Bay was considered an ideal location for one of the Company's bases, to grow food for its crews and serve as a repair station and hospital. Jan van Riebeeck, a 33-year-old surgeon and Company employee, was charged with setting up the post.

Van Riebeeck built a small mud fort on the site where the Castle of Good Hope now stands, and established the nearby Company's Garden to grow fresh fruit and vegetables – now a popular park in the heart of the city. After plans to work the land with local Khoikhoi labour foundered, slaves were imported from the East Indies. In 1666, the foundations were laid for a much larger fort, and the pentagonal Castle of Good

Hope was built. These early years are chronicled in the Military Museum at the castle (see page 28).

The settlement spread into the surrounding country-side, as grain farming began near what is now the suburb of Rondebosch, and, to expand further, some of the Dutch East India Company's servants were allowed to become independent farmers. The land, which had for so long been the sole domain of the San and the Khoikhoi, became the property of the Dutch, with Van Riebeeck laying claim to an area near what is now Wynberg, where in 1658 he planted the first large-scale vineyard in South Africa.

The Khoikhoi attempted to expel the Europeans in 1659, but they failed. With the subsequent influx of French and German immigrants in the early 18th century displacing them further, Khoikhoi society began to fall apart, and was decimated by a smallpox epidemic in 1713. The nomadic San moved further afield, but were often attacked by settlers. Some were even shot and stuffed by trophy hunters. Many San and Khoikhoi eventually intermingled, their descendants becoming part of what is known today as the coloured population.

Governor Simon van der Stel was an important influence on the Cape in the latter part of the 17th century. He founded the South African wine industry, building some of the most beautiful mansions and great estates in the Western Cape. Many fine examples of these supremely elegant Cape Dutch buildings still remain.

From 1680 onwards, religious refugees began to arrive from Europe, including Huguenots from France, who planted vineyards around what became known as Franschhoek.

By 1750 the original tiny settlement founded by Van Riebeeck was a small town named Kaapstad – Cape Town – that had over 2,500 inhabitants. A second port opened at Simon's Bay (today's Simon's Town), providing a far safer refuge than the turbulent Table Bay, where shipwrecks were all too common and countless lives were lost to the sea.

BRITISH INFLUENCE

In 1795, Britain seized control of Cape Town, and thus the sea route to the East, at the Battle of Muizenberg. Under British rule, the monopolies imposed by the Dutch East India Company to protect its own interests were abolished, and much freer trade began. Cape Town became a sea port of international importance, and the town's cosmopolitan character was firmly established.

Cape Town in 1680

The Cape was returned to the Dutch in 1803, but the British regained control at the Battle of Blaauwberg (1806), and it formally became a British colony in 1814. Major companies established offices here, and within a few short years much of the infrastructure that supported the historic city centre was in place. In 1815, the first postal packet service began, with ships sailing between Cape Town and England. This eventually led to the first passenger cruise liners, and was the start of the long-standing association between the city and the Union-Castle shipping line, whose old Cape headquarters now house the Maritime Museum at the V&A Waterfront.

The small settlements around Cape Town started to grow. Simon's Town became home to the navy, and developed a thriving fishing and whaling industry. Under the influence of talented architects such as Louis Michel Thibault and the sculptor Anton Anreith – both of whom had arrived as soldiers and begun working here during the VOC period – houses and commercial buildings of enduring beauty were built. Anreith's fine work is evident throughout the region, with examples including the Castle of Good Hope's ornate Kat Balcony and the nearby Groote Kerk's pulpit.

In 1834 slavery was abolished by the British, and religious freedom was granted. This wasn't an entirely altruistic move; it cost more to keep slaves than to pay wages. The primarily Muslim ex-slaves established their own close community in Cape Town's Bo-Kaap neighbourhood.

THE CITY EVOLVES

In the 1860s, building work started on the Victoria and Alfred docks to meet the pressing need for a safe harbour for the numerous cargo ships now making port at Cape Town.

By the end of the 19th century, Cape Town had changed beyond recognition, its streets lined with banks and commercial buildings, fine mansions and large department stores. The discovery of diamonds around present-day Kimberley, followed by gold in the Witwatersrand (Johannesburg), led to the building of railways linking what was now a substantial city to other rapidly developing areas of Africa. Cecil John Rhodes, whose statue at the University of Cape Town (UCT) sparked 2015's #RhodesMustFall protests, typifies this period of colonial development. The arch colonialist and prime minister of the Cape (1890–96) built a splendid estate at Rondebosch, and bequeathed to the nation the vast plot of land at the foot of Table Mountain that would become the world-famous Kirstenbosch National Botanical Garden.

In 1910, eight years after the end of the bloody Anglo-Boer Wars, the opposing sides – the British and the Dutch-speaking Boers, the ancestors of today's Afrikaners – came together to form the Union of South Africa. Cape Town became the legislative capital of the newly unified country, a role it fulfils to this day.

A whites only sign at a Cape Town beach

THE APARTHEID ERA

Although African cooperation had helped the British to victory, Africans did not benefit from the unification of South Africa. The new government began to issue decrees from the Houses of Parliament in Cape Town that eroded the rights of non-whites. From 1913, their right to own property was severely restricted, and from 1936 they were unable to vote.

When the National Party came to power in 1948 under D.F. Malan, it pledged to introduce influx control, to stop what was felt to be excessive numbers of black workers moving to major cities. It would eventually bring in nationwide, compulsory, racial segregation, embedding the abhorrent apartheid regime.

By the 1960s, African workers were concentrated in the grim shanty towns and men-only hostels of the Cape Flats, forbidden to bring their families to live with them. A peaceful demonstration in Cape Town by inhabitants of the Langa township in 1960 resulted in the deaths of three protestors, who were shot by police, fuelling the armed struggle against this oppression. High-profile opponents of apartheid, including Nelson Mandela and Walter Sisulu, were sentenced to lengthy incarceration on Robben Island, a bleak island prison in Table Bay, Cape Town.

Nelson Mandela in 1990

The Group Areas Act of 1966 further oppressed the city's African and coloured communities, forcibly evicting them from their homes in newly designated 'white areas' to the outlying Cape Flats. In 1972, coloured representation on the town council was abolished and, in 1976, Johannesburg's brutal Soweto uprising was a nadir for South Africa.

A NEW START

In the 1980s, Cape Town, like all of South Africa, underwent tremendous change as the fight against apartheid took hold. The strongest anti-apartheid force yet, the United Democratic Front, was formed on the Cape Flats in 1983. In protest against the violent oppression suffered by the non-whites, many countries imposed harsh economic sanctions on South Africa. These proved crippling, hugely damaging Cape Town by depriving it of the cargo ships that were its lifeblood. South Africans were banned from international sporting events – a particularly wounding blow to such a sports-loving country – and the cultural boycott saw big-name musicians skip South Africa on world tours.

In 1986 history was made at St George's Cathedral, Cape Town, when Desmond Tutu was enthroned as South Africa's first black archbishop. In 1989, Tutu led the 30,000-strong Peace March from the same spot, and coined the term

'Rainbow Nation' when he addressed the crowd outside City Hall.

The city became the focus of the eyes of the world in 1990, when, in a surprise initiative by President F.W. de Klerk, Nelson Mandela was released after 27 years in prison. Within hours of his release, Mandela stood on the balcony of City Hall,

⊙ NELSON MANDELA

Born to a local chief in the Eastern Cape in 1918, Mandela's given name was Rolihlahla ('Troublemaker'), but he acquired the 'Christian' name of Nelson upon becoming the first member of his family to attend school. Politically active while he studied law, Mandela and fellow lawyers Oliver Tambo and Walter Sisulu formed the ANC Youth League in 1944.

Mandela was committed to peaceful protest in the early years of his activist career, but that changed after the police massacre of 69 protesters at Sharpeville in 1960 and subsequent banning of the ANC, which led to his formation and leadership of Umkhonto we Sizwe (Spear of the Nation), the ANC's military wing. In 1964, Mandela was sentenced to life imprisonment for high treason, and he was incarcerated on Robben Island.

In February 1990, President de Klerk lifted the ban on the ANC and Mandela made his first public appearance in 26 years outside Cape Town's City Hall. Ensuing negotiations led to a joint Nobel Peace Prize with de Klerk in 1993, and to the far bigger prize of leading the ANC to victory in South Africa's first fully democratic election in May 1994.

Mandela retired as president in 1999, and passed away in 2013 at the age of 95, but the man nicknamed 'Madiba' remains a beloved figurehead for South Africans of all races and creeds.

addressing a crowd of over 100,000 standing on Grand Parade below him. This historical moment was witnessed by millions of people on televisions all over the world.

Four years later, Nelson Mandela became the first black president of South Africa, and from the Parliament in Cape Town, began the delicate process of peaceful reconciliation after centuries of racial conflict. Today the 'Mother City' continues to play a crucial role in the welfare of her country, with all laws emanating from the city's Houses of Parliament.

DEMOCRACY & DROUGHT

The tiny settlement established in 1652 is now one of the most important centres of commerce on the African continent. The city hosted several games in the 2010 FIFA World Cup, for which the stadium in Green Point was built.

For many years, the Democratic Alliance (DA) party set an example for the rest of the country with its management of Cape Town and the Western Cape under provincial premier Helen Zille. It also won votes in other provinces from the ruling ANC (African National Congress), as the party of Mandela and Oliver Tambo saw its star fade during the years of wanton corruption that characterised Jacob Zuma's presidency (2009–18). However, the DA became overshadowed in Cape Town by infighting with its provincial leader and mayor, Patricia de Lille, who was accused of corruption and eventually left to form her own party, For Good. At the same time it had the challenge of the severe drought that hit Cape Town, but the threat of becoming the world's first major city to run out of water has made Capetonians water conscious. Visitors will find many taps switched off and signs advising them to 'let it mellow'.

HISTORICAL LANDMARKS

1488 Bartolomeu Dias rounds the Cape of Good Hope.

1498 Vasco da Gama discovers the Spice Route to India.

1503 Antonio de Saldanha names Table Mountain.

1652 Jan van Riebeeck establishes a trading post at Table Bay.

1658 Slaves first brought to the Cape. First large-scale vineyard planted.

1680s German and French Huguenot settlers arrive.

1795 The British take control of Cape Town at the Battle of Muizenberg.

1803 Cape Town given back to the Dutch.

1806 The British retake the Cape at the Battle of Blaauwberg.

1814 Congress of Vienna cedes the Cape to the British.

1834 Slavery abolished.

1880 Railways now link Cape Town to much of the African subcontinent.

1910 The Union of South Africa is established.

1948 The National Party comes to power, introducing apartheid.

1960 Police kill anti-apartheid protestors during demonstrations.

1964 Nelson Mandela is imprisoned on Robben Island.

1966 Group Areas Act relocates African and coloured communities to the Cape Flats.

1986 Desmond Tutu becomes first black Archbishop of Cape Town.

1990 Mandela released from prison.

1994 Mandela's ANC wins the country's first democratic election.

1996 Truth and Reconciliation Commission chaired by Archbishop Desmond Tutu begins hearings on human rights crimes committed during apartheid.

2006 South Africa becomes the first African country – and the fifth in the world – to allow same-sex unions.

2009 Jacob Zuma elected President of South Africa.

2010 South Africa hosts the FIFA World Cup.

2013 Nelson Mandela dies.

2017 Cyril Ramaphosa succeeds Zuma as ANC leader, and subsequently President of South Africa.

2018 Dan Plato succeeds Patricia de Lille as mayor of drought-struck Cape Town.

View from the Zeitz Museum of
Contemporary Art Africa

WHERE TO GO

Cape Town is a joy to explore. The historic city centre is small in size and easy to walk around, while the neighbouring Victoria and Alfred Waterfront, a beautifully restored and pedestrianised harbour area, bustles with energy and life day and night. Ever-present Table Mountain provides a spectacular backdrop to the city and even more spectacular views from its summit. As if the city's attractions weren't enough, within a short drive, Uber or Baz Bus ride lie a wealth of natural wonders, including Cape Point, the Winelands and the Garden Route.

CITY CENTRE

Cape Town's city centre is laid out on a grid system, and it is easy to find your way around, and is mostly safe during the day. Numerous tours and historic walks are available, but you can easily make your own itinerary. You can see most of the historic highlights in just half a day's easy walking, while a relatively undemanding day's exploring will really give you a good sense of the place. Be aware, though, that the African sun can get very hot, so take your time, wear a hat and drink lots of water.

AROUND THE CASTLE OF GOOD HOPE

The **Castle of Good Hope** Ⓐ (daily 9am–5pm; www.castle-ofgoodhope.co.za) on Castle Street is the oldest surviving European building in South Africa. This pentagonal fort, which underwent extensive restoration over 1969–93, replaced the original wooden fortress established by Jan van Riebeeck as the local headquarters of the Dutch East India Company. It took 13 years to construct, and was finished in 1679. For 150 years

District 6 Museum

the Castle was the heart of administrative, social and economic life at the Cape. Today it still retains an active military purpose, as the regimental headquarters for the Cape Town Highlanders of the South African National Defence Force (SANDF).The military Key Ceremony takes place on weekdays at 10am and noon, with a firing of the cannon at 10am, 11am and noon Monday to Saturday. Viewed from the outside, the Castle is unimpressive, but its merit lies in its historical interest.

Three museums are housed here. The Military Museum relates the story of the early years of the Dutch East India Company's presence at the Cape; the rooms of the Secunde's House, originally the home of the deputy governor, are furnished in the style of the 16th and 17th centuries; and the marvellous William Fehr Collection of paintings, furniture, china and porcelain in the Governor's Residence is well worth a visit. This last building is adorned by the Kat Balcony, with its ornate sculpture by Anton Anreith. Free official tours (included in the admission charge) are given around the ramparts, dungeon, torture chamber and armouries, starting at 11am, noon, 2pm, 3pm and 4pm daily, and there is a café in the courtyard.

Opposite the Castle, across Castle Street, lies **Grand Parade**, where vast crowds gathered to hear Nelson Mandela's first speech upon being released from prison. A lively flea market operates here every Wednesday and Saturday.

City Hall Ⓑ, with the balcony where Mandela made that historic speech, is on Darling Street. Built in the Italian Renaissance style in 1905, it is home to the Cape Town Philharmonic Orchestra. Entrance is free to view this splendid example of Edwardian opulence, with its ornate stained-glass window. The neighbouring Old Drill Hall, built in the 1880s, houses the Central Library.

District Six, south of the Castle of Good Hope, was once a multicultural neighbourhood, with some 60,000 predominantly Coloured inhabitants forming a lively community. However, it could not withstand the apartheid-era Group Areas Act. In 1966 it was designated a White Group Area, and all non-whites were forcibly evicted from their homes and relocated to the more recently established townships on the less central Cape Flats. Over the next 15 years, the buildings of District Six were systematically reduced to rubble. Most of the houses due to take their place were never built, so strong was the national and international outrage at the demolition of the original community, although Cape Peninsula University of Technology is located here. Local artists, musicians, novelists and playwrights such as David Kramer still wistfully remember this lost Harlem of the Cape, and you can get a sense of what it might have been like on the dilapidated side streets of nearby Woodstock.

Today the land remains largely undeveloped, and the story of the uprooted residents is told in the intensely moving **District Six Museum Ⓒ** (Mon–Sat 9am–4pm; www.districtsix.co.za) based in the former Buitenkant Street Methodist Church. Photographs, original street signs and written recollections of past inhabitants bear vivid witness to the devastating impact of apartheid. There is an excellent bookshop at the museum as well as a coffee

Trafalgar Place Flower Market

shop. The museum also offers guided tours of both the exhibits and the area that was formerly District Six, led by ex-residents, though the neighbourhood tours must be booked in advance.

ADDERLEY STREET

At the west end of Darling Street is **Adderley Street**, named in honour of Charles Adderley, a 19th-century British politician. He earned the gratitude of the residents of Cape Town by helping them resist attempts by the British government to establish a penal colony at the Cape. Once a prestigious residential area with oak-shaded sidewalks for prominent local families, Adderley Street is now a major commercial thoroughfare.

Don't miss the vivid, gloriously scented blooms in the **Trafalgar Place Flower Market** – and enjoy the lively banter of the Bo-Kaap women as you browse.

A little further along on the left is the Mother Church of the Dutch Reformed faith, the **Groote Kerk**, entered from Church Square. Here, the important Afrikaans families of Cape Town worshipped in the second half of the 19th century, and one can view the enclosed pews. Each has its own door, so social distinctions could be maintained, even at prayer. A church has existed here since 1678, but the present building was erected in 1841. The enormous carved pulpit by sculptor Anton Anreith and carpenter Jan Graaff was originally installed in the previous church on this site. Crafted from Burmese teak, with lion-shaped supports made from stinkwood, it is truly outstanding.

At the top (Table Mountain) end of Adderley Street, the **Slave Lodge D** (Mon–Sat 9am–5pm; www.iziko.org.za) was built in 1679 to provide cramped accommodation for the hundreds of slaves who worked in the adjacent Company's Garden. It later became a brothel, then served somewhat different purposes from 1810, as government offices, the Supreme Court, the country's first library and first post office. This handsome two-storey building now houses a series of harrowing but fascinating multimedia displays charting the local and international history of the slave trade. Outside is a statue of Jan Smuts (1870–1950), who fought against the British in the Second Anglo-Boer War, with them in both World Wars and was twice Prime Minister of South Africa.

St George's Cathedral E, nearby on Wale Street, was the religious seat of Desmond Tutu during his tenure as Archbishop of Cape Town from 1986 to 1995. From here, in 1989, he led 30,000 people to City Hall, where he famously declared to the world, 'We are the rainbow people!' Southern Africa's oldest cathedral, today's early-20th-century building owes its Gothic appearance to architect Sir Herbert Baker (1862–1946), who revamped the original 1834 cathedral.

AROUND LONG STREET

Parallel with and just west of Adderley Street is **St George's Mall**, a busy promenade lined with shops, stalls and cafés, where street entertainers perform for the crowds. There are good grazing opportunities at the weekly **Earth Fair Food Market** (Thu 11am–3pm; www.earthfairmarket.co.za) at the Wale Street end. Just off St George's Mall, the busking and browsing fun continues on cobbled **Greenmarket Square F**. The scene of many public announcements, including that of the abolition of slavery in 1834, it is now a colourful, busy souvenir market, where you can bargain for African masks, carvings, fabrics and jewellery.

The **Old Town House** Ⓖ (9am–4pm daily; www.iziko.org.za) on Greenmarket Square was built in 1755 as the headquarters of the Burgher Watch, effectively an early combined police force and fire department. This beautiful example of Cape Rococo architecture, once the most important civic building in Cape Town, is now an art gallery, home to the Michaelis Collection of 17th-century Dutch and Flemish paintings.

Long Street Ⓗ is a fascinating mix of bygone elegance and more recent sleaziness combined with architectural diversity. Elaborate Cape Georgian and Victorian houses with ornate wroughtiron balconies echo the architecture of New Orleans' French Quarter, and provide first-floor vantage points for a coffee or cocktail.

Situated at 40 Long Street, the **South African Missionary Meeting House Museum** (Mon–Fri 9am–4pm; free) is an oasis of calm on this otherwise bustling road. The country's first missionary church, this pretty peach-and-white building, constructed in 1804, now contains exhibits portraying the history of mission work in South Africa, with particular reference to the literacy and religious education it offered to slaves.

Near the northern end of Long Street, just around the corner at 35 Strand Street, is the **Koopmans de Wet House** (Thu & Fri 9am–4pm; www.iziko.org.za). Extravagantly decorated rooms furnished in late 18th-century European style stand in stark contrast to the slave quarters.

On the other side of Long Street, at 98 Strand Street, is South Africa's first **Lutheran Church** Ⓘ. Under the Dutch East India Company, German immigrants were supposed to worship in the Dutch Reformed Church, and merchant Martin Melck celebrated their religious emancipation in the 1770s by funding this splendid church. Next to the church is the Martin Melck House, a fine original townhouse also dating from the late 18th century; together they form South Africa's oldest city block.

Long Street architecture

GOVERNMENT AVENUE

The leafy pedestrian walkway of **Government Avenue**, extending south from the top of Adderley Street, forms the heart of the historic centre of Cape Town. On the left, with the main entrance on Parliament Street, lie the **Houses of Parliament** (www.parliament.gov.za), scene of so many dramatic events in the turbulent history of South Africa. Tickets to watch parliamentary sessions or tour the buildings are available.

De Tuynhuys, the official office of the President of South Africa, is next door to the Houses of Parliament. Originally the Guest House for the Dutch East India Company, it was remodelled extensively by a succession of governors to become the fine building you see today. In 1992, President F.W. de Klerk stood outside and announced that South Africa had 'closed the book on apartheid'.

The 3 hectares (7 acres) of well-tended parkland you see in the **Company's Garden** are all that remain of the original 17 hectares (43 acres). Today it is a beautiful botanical garden.

Next up is the **Delville Wood Memorial**, where Alfred Turner and Anton van Wouw sculptures commemorate the 2,300 South African casualties at the Battle of Delville Wood in France during World War I. Overlooking this is the country's largest and oldest museum, the **South African Museum**  (daily 9am–5pm; www.iziko.org.za). A magnificent building with Table Mountain as its backdrop, this is a truly wonderful place, with plenty to interest both young and old. It is primarily dedicated to natural history. Notable exhibits include dioramas of prehistoric life and a four-storey-high Whale Well, visible from all floors. The latter contains a huge, 20.5m-long skeleton of a blue whale. The anthropological exhibits are not to be missed either, including remarkable depictions of 19th–century San tribal life, and some truly superb rock art.

The **Planetarium** adjoining the Museum has daily shows, some specifically for children, providing an excellent opportunity to learn more about the night sky of the southern hemisphere.

Across Government Avenue from the South African Museum you will find the eclectic **South African National Gallery** (daily 9am–5pm; www.iziko.org.za). This originally displayed mainly European art, and still contains a

Statue of Cecil Rhodes in Company's Garden

number of works by renowned artists such as Gainsborough and Reynolds. However, the primary focus is now on modern and contemporary South African art, and there is a growing collection of traditional tribal work, including carvings and beadwork.

On nearby Hatfield Street, the **South African Jewish Museum** (Sun–Thu 10am–5pm, Fri 10am–2pm; closed on Jewish holidays; www.sajewishmuseum.co.za) is partly housed in the oldest synagogue in the country. The history of Jewish life in South Africa is chronicled through photographs, art, books, artefacts and interactive displays in this opulent building. In the same complex is the harrowing **Holocaust & Genocide Centre** (www.ctholocaust.co.za; Sun–Thu 10am–5pm, Fri 10am–2pm; free, donations appreciated), which documents the history of European anti-Semitism and touches on the Nazi influence on the South African National Party that engineered apartheid. Bring your passport or photo ID to access the complex, which also includes the impressive Great Synagogue (or Gardens Shul) dating to 1905.

Across Orange Street at the far end of Government Avenue is a Cape Town landmark: the sugar-pink **Mount Nelson Hotel**, the most prestigious hotel in the city. With its grand, white-pedimented gateway, 'the Nellie' has been an integral part of city life since 1899. The buffet breakfast or afternoon tea on its garden terrace is a memorable and civilised occasion.

BO-KAAP

On the slopes of Signal Hill, roughly bounded by Leeuwen, Buitengracht and Strand streets, is the **Bo-Kaap** Ⓝ (literally 'Upper Cape'), the traditional home of Cape Town's Muslim community. It is a fascinating place, with 18th- and early 19th-century 'cube' houses painted in colourful shades, narrow streets, spice shops, and the minarets of 10 mosques, including South Africa's first official mosque, the Auwal (on Dorp Street).

The inhabitants of the Bo-Kaap are mostly descended from highly skilled and educated slaves and Islamic dissidents, shipped from the East Indies by the Dutch. They brought with them their faith, Sufism (part of the Islamic religion), and a strong culture that has survived centuries of repression, when their language, history and writing could only be preserved in secret. Although the Cape Muslims are still sometimes erroneously referred to as the 'Cape Malays', few of their ancestors actually came from Malaysia. Traders at that time used the Malay language as a common tongue, hence the name Cape Malay, which is still applied to the distinctive cuisine developed by this community.

Until 1834 this area was inhabited by Dutch and English artisans, but when slavery was abolished, the freed Muslims moved in. They established a community that, unlike District Six, survived even the notorious Group Areas Act of 1966. Under this, virtually every non-white neighbourhood in Cape Town was designated a White Group Area, and razed to the ground to make way for whites-only housing. The original inhabitants were forcibly relocated out of the city to the Cape Flats.

The **Bo-Kaap Museum** (Mon–Sat 9am–4pm, closed on Islamic holidays; www.iziko.org.za) at 71 Wale Street is based around the fine house and possessions of a wealthy 19th-century Muslim family, with exhibits depicting the history of the community.

Today Bo-Kaap is a friendly neighbourhood, but tensions have been caused by property developers buying and building here, amid locals' fears that their culture and community will be lost. To get the most out of a visit it is a good idea to take a guided tour, which may also give you the opportunity to meet some of the area's

inhabitants or even experience a Cape Malay cooking workshop (and meal) in the kitchen of one of its local residents.

VICTORIA AND ALFRED WATERFRONT

The **Victoria and Alfred (V&A) Waterfront** ⓞ (daily 9am–6pm, though some shops open until 9pm and some restaurants stay open to midnight; free; tel: 021-408 7600; www.waterfront. co.za) – or plain 'Waterfront', as locals call it – is one of Cape Town's most popular and vibrant attractions. The Waterfront's main areas are the Quays District (including the Victoria Wharf, Watershed and Two Oceans Aquarium) and, over the footbridge, the Clock Tower and Silo Districts. At its heart are the marina and Victoria and Alfred Basins, the latter named after Queen Victoria's second son, Prince Alfred. In 1860, he ceremonially tipped the first rock to begin construction of the harbour, which had become essential when insurer Lloyds of London refused to cover ships docking in Table Bay.

The V&A Waterfront's historic warehouses and dock buildings have been beautifully restored and contain some of the city's best shops, nightspots and restaurants, along with several museums, an aquarium, a craft market,

Colourful houses in Bo-Kaap

V&A Waterfront

two cinemas, a comedy club and a microbrewery. It is also the site of the Nelson Mandela Gateway, the departure point for all ferry tours to Robben Island, while private operators run helicopter and boat trips around the harbour and along the coastline.

The V&A Waterfront is a convenient spot to buy everything from souvenirs to sunglasses. The main mall is the **Victoria Wharf Shopping Centre**. One of the smartest shopping malls in the country, it is a magnet for locals and tourists alike. Shops and stalls sell both local and international fashion labels, plus diamond jewellery, books, groceries and more. The nearby **Watershed** offers African craftwork and local design in an upmarket environment. Between the Victoria Wharf and Watershed, **Market Square** is an open space for fairs and events in season. To one side is the **Amphitheatre**, a venue for street theatre and buskers, and a popular meeting point. In the same area is Nobel Square, with bronze statues of South Africa's four Nobel Peace Prize winners: Nelson Mandela, Desmond Tutu, F.W. de Klerk and the former president of the ANC, Chief Albert John Lutuli.

The maritime history of the Cape is detailed in full at the **Maritime Centre** (daily 9am–4pm; www.iziko.org.za) on the first floor of Union Castle House on Dock Road. Exhibits give an overview of shipping in Cape Town and illustrate Table Bay from the

17th century onwards; several superb models include a splendid depiction of Cape Town Harbour as it appeared in 1886.

Other attractions reflecting the area's maritime past include the **Time Ball Tower**, once used by navigators in the bay to set their clocks, and the pedestrian swing-bridge that leads over to the old **Clock Tower**. Built as the Port Captain's office in 1883, the tower overlooks Victoria Basin and marks the original entrance to the docks. With its pointed windows and little pinnacled belfry, it has a distinctly Gothic look.

The V&A Waterfront is still an active harbour, and fishing boats, yachts and cruise liners are all to be seen there. Take to the water yourself on a boat tour and look for Cape fur seals enjoying the waves or sunning themselves on the docks by the Clock Tower. A host of cruises, sailing, fishing and diving excursions can be taken from the Waterfront, mostly from the quays alongside Victoria Wharf.

The **Two Oceans Aquarium** Ⓟ (daily 9.30am–6pm; feeding times: penguins 11.30am and 2.30pm, sea turtles, rays and guitarfish noon and 2pm, ragged-tooth sharks Sun 3pm; tel: 021-418 3823; www.aquarium.co.za) showcases the unique eco-system of the Cape Peninsula, with its extraordinary bounty of fish, birds, mammals, reptiles and plant life from the Indian and Atlantic oceans. Stunning exhibits include a vast, mesmerising tank containing rays, turtles, musselcrackers and more in 1.6 million litres of water; a psychedelic hall of jellyfish; a predator tank with ragged-tooth sharks, giant yellowtail and yellowbelly rockcod; and a kelp forest. There is also a fun children's play area with a window onto the penguin pool, as well as touch pools allowing visitors to examine some of the friendlier creatures firsthand. Qualified scuba-divers can swim among the ragged-tooth sharks in the Predator Exhibit, or you can take a PADI course here and dive among rays on the same day. Children also

The Clock Tower

enjoy **Scratch Patch** (daily 9am–5pm; www.scratch-patch.co.za). The inspiration behind this place is the amazing variety of minerals in South Africa. You can have fun picking out your favourite stones from the colourful heaps scattered about, have them weighed, then take them home and keep them in deep bowls on the coffee table.

TABLE MOUNTAIN

Standing 1,086m (3,500ft plus) tall and measuring nearly 3km (2 miles) across, **Table Mountain** (www.tmnp.co.za) was declared a National Monument in 1957 and became the centrepiece of an eponymous national park covering most uninhabited parts of the Cape Peninsula. The mountain is also part of the Cape Floral Kingdom Unesco World Heritage Site.

No visit to Cape Town is complete without taking in the unforgettable bird's-eye views from the summit of Hoerikwaggo (Mountain in the Sea), as the Khoikhoi called Table Mountain. All facets of city life are spread out below in miniature – ships in the bay, fine houses in wealthy suburbs, beautiful beaches, historic buildings, soaring skyscrapers and the distant townships of the Cape Flats.

The weather at the top of the mountain can change very quickly. One moment it is in sparkling sunshine, the next, shrouded in cloud – the 'Tablecloth' that sits on top and spills down over the edges. If you want to go up the mountain, the golden rule is that if you can see the top, go now!

The brief but exhilarating cable-car ride to the top of Table Mountain is, in itself, an adventure to be treasured. The original **Cableway** (May–Aug daily 8.30am–6pm, Sep–Apr longer hours; tel: 021-424 8181; www.tablemountain.net) opened in 1929 and proved immediately popular. Over 900,000 visitors a year choose to travel to the summit in this way, and to meet this demand, the latest technology was imported from Switzerland in 1997. The cable cars revolve 360° in the course of the journey, ensuring that all passengers enjoy every part of the panorama. Letters bearing the Table Mountain postmark can be sent from the souvenir shop at the summit, where

---

⊙ CULTURAL CAPE TOWN

Adding a new dimension to the Waterfront and putting Cape Town on the cultural map, the **Zeitz MOCAA** (Museum of Contemporary Art Africa; Wed–Mon 10am–6pm; tel: 087-350 4777; www.zeitzmocaa.museum) occupies what was once Sub-Saharan Africa's tallest building. From its dramatic entrance hall to 80 galleries exhibiting contemporary art from across Africa, the museum has turned a former grain silo into a long-awaited world-class platform for African art on home territory. There is a café and sculpture garden up top, as well as one of South Africa's best boutique hotels, the **Silo Hotel** (www.theroyalportfolio.com), where non-guests can access the rooftop bar. The **Silo District**, a cultural quarter of galleries, boutiques, restaurants and the Radisson Red hotel, has developed around the museum since it opened in 2017. You can access it up the steps from the Clock Tower District.

paved paths lead along the plateau edge to viewing platforms and a self-service restaurant.

The Cableway operates daily, weather permitting, departing from the Lower Cableway Station every few minutes. To shorten your queueing time, get there early and, most importantly, buy tickets in advance – either online, from the Lower Cableway Station or from an office of Cape Town Tourism or City Sightseeing tour buses.

The indigenous flora and fauna to be found here are truly memorable. Table Mountain is home to almost 1,500 species of plants, some found nowhere else in the world, and the renowned Kirstenbosch National Botanical Garden runs down from its eastern flank. Whatever the season, you are sure to see stunning fynbos and flowers in a glorious range of colours, including proteas and Silver Trees. Wildlife is also plentiful, including porcupines, the rodent-like dassie (or rock hyrax, an unlikely relative of the African elephant), grysboks (small, nocturnal antelopes) and baboons. Give baboons a wide berth, leave your car locked with the windows up and ensure food is buried in your bag; click on 'security alerts and safety tips' on the Table Mountain website for more on baboon encounters and updates on mugging hotspots. Following a spate of muggings, footpaths around Devil's Peak and the Southern Peninsula were best avoided at the time of writing. For more on baboons, visit www.baboonmatters.org.za, the website of advocacy organisation Baboon Matters.

There are hundreds of footpaths on the mountain, ranging from straightforward ascents to those best tackled only by experts, and it is a sensible precaution to contact the Mountain Club of South Africa (tel: 021-937 0300; www.mcsa.org.za) or a reputable local tour operator if you are planning a lengthy hike. In emergencies, call 021-480 7700 from mobile phones or 107

from landlines. In the early morning the mountain's western slopes are in shade, making climbing a much cooler experience on trails such as Kasteelpoort, which starts in Camps Bay. The most popular trail is Platteklip, which ploughs up the front of the mountain, while Skeleton Gorge and Nursery Ravine ascend from Kirstenbosch.

Table Mountain is flanked by smaller mountains. To the right, when viewed from the city, are **Lion's Head** and **Signal Hill**, and to the left, **Devil's Peak**. The west face of Table Mountain comprises a series of distinctive rock formations called the **Twelve Apostles**. On a clear day you can see the entire city, V&A Waterfront and Table Bay to the north, Camps Bay and the Twelve Apostles to the west, the mountains of Stellenbosch and the Cape Flats townships to the east, and sometimes even Cape Point to the south, all from within 100m (325ft) of the upper cable-car station. A walk along the plateau gives views of the Southern Suburbs down to False Bay in the south.

The views of the city and Table Mountain from Signal Hill Road, which links Lion's Head to Signal Hill, are also outstanding. Signal Hill was originally a signalling post for communication with ships out at sea, and the Noon Gun is still fired from here each day. For an atmospheric sunset view of the city centre and atlantic suburbs, drive up Signal Hill in the late afternoon.

SOUTHERN SUBURBS

The lush suburbs south of Cape Town extend east from the slopes of Table Mountain and south towards the False Bay coast, with hotels and guest houses in safe neighbourhoods, as well as shopping, restaurants and entertainment options. From their comfortable streets, rich in fine Cape Dutch and Victorian houses, it is easy to get to vineyards, forests and gardens of tremendous beauty, yet they are just 20 minutes' drive from the heart of the city.

KIRSTENBOSCH NATIONAL BOTANICAL GARDEN

The fabulous **Kirstenbosch National Botanical Garden** ❶ (daily Apr–Aug 8am–6pm, Sept–Mar 8am–7pm; tel: 021-799 8783; www. sanbi.org), south of the suburb of Newlands, contains one of the world's most important botanical collections. It was founded in 1913 by Professor Henry Pearson. Few places on the planet are as rich in floral variety as the Western Cape, and these magnificent gardens contain over 7,000 species of native wild plants in an awe-inspiring location under the watchful eye of Table Mountain.

You can easily spend a full day here, following the numerous walking trails. They lead you through densely planted areas alive with scent and colour, past pools stained brown with fynbos, across verdant lawns and up the rocky slopes of Table Mountain to treelined ravines. Other highlights include herb and fragrance gardens, pink-flowering protea shrubs (South Africa's national plant), the conservatory, and the prehistoric cycads in a hidden valley of their Jurassic dinosaur contemporaries. The 130m-long Tree Canopy Walkway, nicknamed the Boomslang (tree snake) for its serpentine appearance,

Table Mountain Cableway and Lion's Head

has become Kirstenbosch's chief attraction since it opened, 12m above the Arboretum, in 2014.

The gardens are definitely a must-see, even if you lack green fingers. Even a few hours spent in their leafy confines will give you an idea of the incredible wealth of flora in this area. There is a charming restaurant and tearoom (inside Gate 2), where you can order a gourmet picnic and even rent a picnic basket, as well a Vida e Caffè coffee shop (at Gate 1), a Moyo restaurant between the two gates, and a nursery and shops selling flowers, succulents, fynbos plants and books. On Sunday evenings during the summer months (November to April), atmospheric open-air concerts take place here, ranging from jazz to classical and attracting performers from local acts to big names such as James and the Pixies. For a lasting memory, enjoy a leisurely picnic and a bottle of crisp white wine in this beautiful setting.

Many of the paths are hilly and the sun can be very hot, so take your time. There is ample shade, though, and a gentle breeze much of the time. The signage within the gardens isn't very good, so it is wise to equip yourself with a map before you wander into this botanical heaven. If you have difficulty walking, golf-cart tours are available, and there is a Braille Trail and free guided tours.

On the last Sunday of each month (except June–August) the Kirstenbosch Craft and Food Market takes place outside the gardens' main gate. Over 200 outdoor stalls sell clothing, ceramics, beadwork and sculptures, as well as some good food, with proceeds from stall rentals going to the gardens.

CONSTANTIA

Nestled into the lower slopes of Table Mountain and Constantiaberg Mountain, and enjoying views of False Bay, **Constantia** was the birthplace of the wine industry in South Africa. Today, the world's oldest winemaking region outside Europe is an affluent suburb with a wine route of nine upmarket estates.

This luscious spot was chosen by the Governor of Cape Town, Simon van der Stel, for his own estate, out of the vast expanse of rich farmland he was given by the Dutch East India Company. Where the governor led, other high-ranking families followed, and consequently Constantia is rich in beautiful old Cape Dutch architecture. Van der Stel planted the first vines on his estate in 1685.

After Van der Stel's death, his estate was divided into three smaller estates and sold. The largest estate, **Groot Constantia** ❷ (daily 9am–6pm; free; www.grootconstantia.co.za), is still an active winery, with the added attraction that it contains the original manor house, which is now a museum. The house was founded by Van der Stel but took its modern shape around 1790–1803 under its then owner, Hendrik Cloete, who also commissioned the Anton Anreith sculpture in the niche. Although badly damaged

The tree top walk at Kirstenbosch

by fire in 1925, it has been meticulously restored to its original state, and is quite beautiful. Wine-tastings and chocolate pairings are available, and there is a good restaurant in the old stables, as well as a host of museums and visitor experiences from cellar tours to audio-guide apps.

The other historic estates in the Constantia Valley are **Steenberg** (www.steenbergfarm.com), **Klein Constantia** (www.kleinconstantia.com), **Constantia Uitsig** (www. uitsig.co.za) and **Buitenverwachting** (literally, 'Beyond Expectation'; www.buiten-verwachting.co.za).

They are all arguably a little less formal than Groot Constantia, but just as pretty, and generally have excellent restaurants and offer wine-tasting sessions, typically from around 9am to 4pm Monday to Friday and 9am–noon on Saturday. The produce of all these vineyards is among the best the Cape has to offer, but the ultimate souvenir has to be Vin de Constance, a modern re-creation of the fine dessert wine so beloved by Napoleon, Baudelaire, Jane Austen and others that won Constantia worldwide fame. Wiped out by the 19th-century phylloxera **aphid** plague, it has been revived by Klein Constantia, Groot Constantia, Buitenverwachting and Constantia Uitsig.

Bordering Steenberg, the Norval Foundation (Wed–Mon 10am–5.15pm; www.norvalfoundation.org) adds a serious dose of culture to Constantia's viticulture with its galleries of modern and contemporary art from across Africa and beyond, contained within a purpose-built building designed by Cape Town's DHK Architects. There is also a sculpture garden and an excellent restaurant.

OTHER SUBURBS

South Africa's most famous artist, Irma Stern (1894–1966), once lived at The Firs (Cecil Road, Rosebank), and this small house is now the excellent **Irma Stern Museum** (Tue–Fri 10am–5pm, Sat 10am–2pm; www.irmastern.co.za). A fantastically versatile and prolific painter, Stern's main claim to fame was that she introduced the European Expressionist concept to African art. The collection includes an absorbing and representative collection of Stern's own work, but also a collection of finely crafted Africana

⊙ CARPETS OF FLOWERS

Though the smallest of the world's six floral kingdoms, the Cape Floral Kingdom is the richest, boasting an incredible 8,600 species of wild plants, 5,800 of which are found nowhere else on earth. The most common vegetation is *Fynbos* ('fine bush'). This comprises three families: *Proteas*, which come in all shapes and sizes, all deeply coloured; *Restios*, the hardy ground cover used for thatching; and the delicate *Ericas*, similar to heather. The Cape comes alive with spring flowers in September and October, with the most spectacular displays drawing massive crowds. Traffic jams build up along routes through vast regions carpeted with brightly coloured blooms as far as the eye can see. Some towns and villages hold wildflower festivals at this time of year to celebrate the natural wonder on their doorstep.

collected during her extensive travels around the continent. The fine **Baxter Theatre Complex** (www.baxter.co.za), one of the most important centres for the arts in Cape Town, is nearby.

Rondebosch, south of Rosebank, is distinguished by a number of particularly elegant 19th-century buildings, including the rather grand **University of Cape Town**. On the slopes of Devil's

Groot Constantia Estate

Peak, you can enjoy tremendous views over the Cape Flats to the Hottentots Holland and Helderberg Mountains from the adjoining coffee shop. Alongside Rhodes Drive is the thatched **Mostert's Mill** (www.mostertsmill.co.za), built by the Dutch in 1796 and now Southern Africa's only working windmill.

Sports fans are drawn to the suburb of Newlands by the **Newlands Cricket and Rugby Stadium**, homes to the Western Cape's provincial cricket and rugby teams, which regularly host domestic and international cricket and rugby matches. The latter was a venue in the 1995 Rugby World Cup, which was held in South Africa and won by the country's national team, the Springboks, who also triumphed in 2007. Their 1995 victory was movingly depicted in the Hollywood film "Invictus" (2009), directed by Clint Eastwood and starring Morgan Freeman and Matt Damon, for its historical significance as a catalyst for bringing all South Africans together, one year after the end of apartheid.

On Boundary Road is a working watermill dating to 1840, the **Josephine Mill** (Mon–Fri 10am–1pm; www.josephinemill.co.za), which still produces flour. There is a museum here and you can buy the flour and products made from it.

Wynberg is the site of the **Maynardville Open-Air Theatre**, which puts on Shakespeare plays on February evenings in Maynardville Park (tel: 021-421 7695; www.maynardville.co.za). See the website for details of concerts and other events happening between January and March. Bordering the park's west side is Wynberg Village, a beautifully preserved conservation area of Cape Georgian and Victorian houses with a strip of upmarket cafés, galleries and boutiques on Wolfe Street.

A drive through the suburbs brings home the great divide between rich and poor that persists in a city struggling to address apartheid's spatial legacy. To the east of the M5 highway lie the bleak expanses of the **Cape Flats**, where black African and coloured people inhabit their own separate areas in a painful continuation of South Africa's segregated past. Life in these townships and informal settlements is harsh, alltoofrequently violent, and conditions squalid, yet visitors are often surprised and heartened by the positive attitude and courage of many of the inhabitants. Tourists wishing to explore the Cape Flats are firmly advised not to travel here alone or at night. The only safe way is via one of the township tours.

ROBBEN ISLAND

Lying 10km (6 miles) off the north coast of Cape Town, **Robben Island ❸** is a vivid and poignant reminder of South Africa's troubled political past, for it was here that opponents of apartheid – most famously, Nelson Mandela and his comrade Walter Sisulu – were held. An integral part of the country's history, it is now a national museum and wildlife reserve, and was made a Unesco World Heritage Site in 1999.

Mandela spent 18 years in the place he described as 'the harshest, most iron-fisted outpost in the South African penal system', and his tiny cell has become a shrine for the tens of thou-

Irma Stern Museum

sands of tourists who visit each year. Once you have seen it, you can only marvel at this remarkable man, and realise what an incredible moment it was when he returned to that cell during the Millennium celebration to light a candle to mark hope for the future.

Robben Island may only be visited on the official guided tours that depart from the Nelson Mandela Gateway at the V&A Waterfront at 9am, 11am, 1pm and, between September and April, 3pm. The tour takes 3 1/2 hours, inclusive of the return ferry trip (tel: 021-413 4200; www.robben-island.org.za). Book well ahead. Other operators offer 'trips to Robben Island', but these only view the island from the boat and do not actually land passengers.

Visitors can see the cells where dozens of inmates endured appalling conditions, the lime quarry where pris-oners damaged their eyesight working in the unremitting glare, and the house where Robert Sobukwe served years of solitary confinement. The leper graveyard and church are

Kids in Khayelitsha

a reminder of the other outcasts sent to this island over the centuries.

Visiting the island is a moving and remarkable experience. The tour guides, ex-inmates, provide a graphic insight into life, or rather existence, inside the prison. At times it is a harrowing experience, yet the guides communicate with humour and a positive attitude that is both humbling and uplifting. Ex-warders now work alongside those who were once interred here. In A-Wing, the prison security intercom system has been ingeniously adapted to relate 'Cell Stories'. You can activate these to hear the voices of former prisoners describing their experiences.

An often neglected aspect of Robben Island is its wildlife, which includes introduced antelope, the country's third-largest breeding colony of African penguins, and over 100 other bird species. In the spring the place is alive with colourful flowers, while the waters offshore teem with abalone (a type of large marine snail) and crayfish. Dolphins and seals are often seen on the boat trip from the mainland.

As the boat leaves at the end of the tour, you may have mixed emotions, but you cannot help feeling a deep admiration for all those who suffered here. That this former purgatory has been transformed into such a remarkable experience is testimony

⊙ TOWNSHIP TOURS

The townships that cover the sandy flats east of Cape Town were created under apartheid, when tens of thousands of 'non-white' Capetonians were forcibly evicted from more central suburbs such as District Six, which were rezoned as 'whites only'. The Cape Flats thus became a hotbed of anti-apartheid feeling, as well as gangs and crime, and it is still unwise to explore unguided.

As a result, 'township tours', led by local residents, are offered by many Cape Town operators. Those that focus on the area's positives as well as its poverty, offering interactions with residents and perhaps a theme such as art, jazz or Xhosa cooking, can be a highly rewarding experience. Tours can be by vehicle, foot or bike. The most commonly visited Cape Flats townships are Langa, the oldest (established 1927) and most central; Gugulethu ('Gugs'), dating to the 1960s; and **Khayelitsha** (established 1983), one of South Africa's largest and fasting growing with a population of around 2.5 million.

Tour operators to consider include 18 Gangster Museum (www.18gm.co.za), Andulela (www.andulela.com), Coffeebeans Routes (www.coffeebeansroutes.com), Juma's Tours (www.townshiparttours.co.za), Maboneng Township Arts Experience (www.maboneng.com) and Vamos (www.vamos.co.za).

Some operators, such as Awol (www.awoltours.co.za) and Afrika Moni (www.suedafrika.net/imizamoyethu), focus instead on the Cape Peninsula townships of Imizamo Yethu (Hout Bay) or Masiphumelele (Kommetjie).

Another great way to see the townships is by staying the night at a bed and breakfast, such as Kopanong (www.kopanong-township.co.za), in Khayelitsha. Book and organise transport in advance, and go during daylight hours to check in.

Guide on Robben Island

to the spirit of all who lived under the malignant apartheid regime.

EXCURSIONS

Another joy of Cape Town is the variety of tempting destinations close by, including the world-famous Garden Route and the Winelands. Whether you have just a day to spare, or the luxury of taking some longer breaks around the Western Cape, you'll be spoilt for choice.

CAPE PENINSULA TO CAPE POINT

A drive to Cape Point (and the Cape of Good Hope), returning to Cape Town via the False Bay coast, makes a superb full-day excursion, incorporating glorious beaches, colourful fishing ports, stunning views of mountains and ocean, and a multitude of indigenous flora and fauna.

Atlantic Coast

Head southwest out of the city centre along the coastal road, past striped **Green Point Lighthouse** (actually in Mouille Point), the oldest in South Africa, and **Clifton**, an area known as 'Millionaires' Row,' with some of the country's most expensive homes. After the chichi beachfront strip of cafés and bars in Camps Bay, the shoreline opens up, giving great views, and the road runs along the

⊘ HISTORY OF ROBBEN ISLAND

By the time Nelson Mandela arrived on Robben Island in 1964, this tiny island had been infamous for its brutality for over three centuries. It housed political opponents of whatever regime was in power, criminals, the insane and lepers alike.

Dutch settlers, who named the island after the robbe (seals) that once bred there, first used it as prison in the 17th century. The earliest political prisoner was a Khoikhoi leader called Autshumato. A succession of political detainees followed, including Muslim holy men, who were the founders of Islam in South Africa and are remembered by the island's *kramat* shrine.

From the mid-1800s the island increasingly served as a hospital and a quarantine station, for both people and animals. This diversification didn't lessen the brutality. Patients lived in terrible conditions, with the chronically sick afforded no more consideration than criminals or political dissidents.

In spite of its notorious past, Robben Island is seen as a positive symbol. Ahmed Kathrada, head of the Ex-Political Prisoners Committee, who spent almost 20 years there, said: 'We want it to reflect the triumph of freedom and human dignity over oppression and humiliation, of courage and determination over weakness, of a new South Africa over the old.'

Clifton beach

foot of the Twelve Apostles. Further along, **Llandudno** ❹ is a small, elite village in an outstanding setting with a gorgeous beach. The coastline is popular with divers, and shipwrecks are visible from the hiking trail to **Sandy Bay** nudist beach.

Continue on Victoria Road to the fishing town of **Hout Bay**. Take time to wander around the Mariner's Wharf complex (www.marinerswharf. co.za), with its fish market and seafood restaurants. You can take a boat trip to see the Cape fur seals and seabirds on Duiker Island (nicknamed Seal Island) or check out the family-friendly aviary and zoo, World of Birds (daily 9am–5pm; www.worldofbirds.org.za).

Chapman's Peak Drive ❺ (www.chapmanspeakdrive.co.za), one of the world's most scenic coastal roads, winds along 10km (6 miles) from Hout Bay to Noordhoek. The road took seven years to carve out of the mountain face and opened in 1922. Now a toll road, it rises to 600m (almost 2,000ft) above the ocean, with several narrow parking spots where you can pull over and admire breathtaking views across Hout Bay and as far south as Kommetjie's Slangkop Lighthouse.

Noordhoek is home to many artists and alternatives, giving this area its nickname, the Lentil Curtain, although gentrification is slowly changing the local community. Noordhoek Farm Village (www.thefarmvillage.co.za) and Imhoff Farm (www.imhofffarm.

co.za), with camels out front, are both good stops for lunch and a browse. The nearby hamlet of **Kommetjie**, at the end of a tidal lagoon, is popular for surfing. Following a spate of muggings on Long Beach, between the two settlements, it's safer to go to the equally stunning Kommetjie Beach.

Nature Reserve

Part of the Table Mountain National Park, the **Cape of Good Hope Nature Reserve** ❻ (daily Oct–Mar 6am–6pm, Apr–Sept 7am–5pm; www.capepoint.co.za) protects 8,000 hectares (20,000 acres) of stunningly beautiful windswept crags and fynbos-clad slopes at the continent's southwestern-most point. It is home to over 1,000 species of indigenous flora, and in the spring hardy wild flowers brave gale-force winds to provide a brilliant show of colour. Wildlife includes the Cape mountain zebra, bontebok, eland and ostriches. Although the baboon population can look entertaining, repeated – and strictly forbidden – feeding by tourists has made them aggressive. You can explore the reserve by car or on foot, but take care when hiking, as the vegetation is home to cobras and puff-adders.

It's around 13km (8 miles) from the entrance to **Cape Point**, where the Flying Dutchman funicular railway runs from the visitors centre to the **Cape Point Lighthouse**. There are spectacular views of the **Cape of Good Hope** and along the Cape. The water smashes against the rocks a dizzying distance below. This 19th-century lighthouse was superseded in 1914 by a more powerful one, which you can follow a footpath to. Marine life includes whales, dolphins and seals. There is a fine seafood restaurant here, Two Oceans, with fantastic views across False Bay. The Reserve also has plenty of picnic spots, including the beaches on the more sheltered east coast, and great walking along miles of empty sands with the occasional shipwreck.

False Bay Coast

Immediately outside the entrance to the Reserve, the private **Cape Point Ostrich Farm** (daily 9.30am–5:30 pm; www.cape-pointostrichfarm.com) offers a fun opportunity to meet and learn about the world's largest bird at close quarters. It is a popular activity with children, while eager souvenir-hunters can pick up all manner of ostrich-derived goods, from hollowed-out giant eggs to plush leatherware, and there is also a restaurant.

From here, the coast road leads north to **Simon's Town** ❼. The historic town has been a major naval base since 1687, for the Dutch, the British and now South Africa, as the **South African Naval Museum** (daily 9.30am–3.30pm; www.simons-town.com) attests. Look out for the statue in Jubilee Square that pays tribute to a Great Dane dog called Just Nuisance, the mascot of British sailors based here during World War II.

Simon's Town's greatest attraction lies just south of the town, at **Boulders Beach** ❽ (daily 8am–5pm, Oct–Mar 8am–6.30pm; www.tmnp.co.za), which now forms part of Table Mountain National Park. Boulders and the adjacent Foxy Beach support a colony of around 3,000 black-and-white **African penguins**, and these delightful, charismatic creatures can be observed swimming, squabbling and waddling around the beach from a series of raised wooden walkways.

Fish Hoek is one of the best whale-watching spots along the Cape Peninsula. From **Jager's Walk**, a concrete walkway which runs towards Simon's Town, it is possible to get incredible views of these magnificent mammals from July to November. The town beach is also a winner for families, with a playground and café at its southern end.

To enjoy some accessible mountaintop wilderness, head off-route along Kommetjie Road to **Silvermine Nature Reserve** (daily 8am–6pm; www.tmnp.co.za), whose fynbos-draped slopes are home to a great diversity of mammals and birds, as well as some spectacular winter-blooming king proteas. The section north of Ou Kaapse Weg, the pass connecting Noordhoek to Tokai, is popular for its mountain-ringed dam, which you can circle on a walking path, stop for a picnic and cool off in the fynbos-stained water. In 1927 ancient burial sites were discovered in the Reserve, in Peers Cave, the walls of which are covered in ancient paintings.

Next up is **Muizenberg**, the haunt of the rich and famous in the 1920s. Many of them built holiday homes and the celebrated British crime writer Agatha Christie learnt to surf here. The diverse architectural styles are fascinating, with fine Edwardian houses contrasting with fishermen's cottages, and a line of colourful Victorian bathing huts, which has become an icon of Cape Town, stands on the long beach. Muizenberg Pavilion is popular with children, who enjoy the waterslide and camel rides. It is also the site of a Sunday morning flea market and a great place to take surfing lessons at Gary's Surf School (www.garysurf.com).

Cape Point

Muizenberg, though once seedy, is now experiencing a renaissance, with slumlords leaving and bohemians returning.

STELLENBOSCH AND THE WINELANDS

Within an hour's drive of Cape Town lie hundreds of vineyards, where wine-tasting can be enjoyed in delightful surroundings. A tour of this scenic region is also a visual delight. White, gabled Cape Dutch houses and farm buildings are set against the bright green of vines in full leaf, and dwarfed by towering mountains. Fine restaurants, antique markets and gourmet food shops abound, while museums give a glimpse of rural colonial life.

South Africa has a long history of wine production. Jan van Riebeeck planted the Cape's first vines in 1659, but things really developed after Huguenot refugees arrived from France in the late 17th century, bringing their winemaking expertise with them. The Western Cape is the key region, producing thousands of individual wines from many hundreds of vineyards. All types of wine are made here, from Méthode Cap Classique (MCC; bubbly) to port, but the country is best-known for its fabulous whites, including Chenin Blanc, and for reds such as Pinotage. This fruity, almost purple wine, made from a unique cross between Pinot Noir and Cinsaut grapes, was developed in Stellenbosch in 1925.

The **Stellenbosch Wine Route** (www.wineroute.co.za) is the oldest and most famous of several throughout the Winelands, each incorporating vineyards of varying sizes. Most wine estates offer tastings, usually from 10am to 4pm on weekdays and over more restricted hours on Saturday and Sunday, and many have restaurants and shops. Smaller, boutique or garagiste operations may only offer tastings by

Braying birds

The African penguin was until recently known as the jackass penguin, in reference to the comic braying call that welcomes visitors to Boulders Beach.

appointment. Following two or three routes, exploring their towns and attractions, can easily take the better part of a week. It is possible to experience many of the pleasures of the Winelands in a day, but taking two days with an overnight stop can make for a more relaxing excursion. It is best to visit in summer, when the vines are in leaf, or late summer to autumn, when the glorious autumn foliage follows harvest time.

Penguins on Boulders Beach

Accommodation in this area is excellent, with many fine small country hotels and guest houses, often in beautiful old buildings, including the oldest country inn in South Africa, **Oude Werf** (www.oudewerf.co.za) in Stellenbosch. Additionally, some vineyards offer farmstays and other overnight accommodation.

Stellenbosch

First settled in 1679, **Stellenbosch** ❾ is the second-oldest town in South Africa. It is now a busy university town, though the leafy historic quarter retains its architectural charm. 'Stellies', as the students call it, was also nicknamed Eikestad (Oak Town) due to the old oaks that line its streets. There are plenty of good shops, restaurants and cafés here, among the lovely Cape Dutch, Georgian and Victorian houses.

Victorian bathing huts, St James beach

The best starting point for a leisurely tour is the oak-shaded village green known as **Die Braak**. The green and its African craft stalls are surrounded by old buildings, notably a Powder House built in 1777, the Anglican Church of St Mary (1852) and the Rhenish Church (1823). A block further south, **Dorp Street** is lined by a series of marvellously ornate Cape Dutch facades, most of which date to the 19th century or earlier. These include a fascinating shop which has changed little over the past century: **Oom Samie Se Winkel** ('Uncle Samie's Store') is packed with handmade crafts, wines, basketry, dried fruit, antiques, lacework and farm implements, evoking the trading posts of yore.

The **Village Museum** (Mon–Sat 9am–5pm, Sun 10am–1pm; www.stelmus.co.za) on Ryneveld Street is a complex of historic houses, depicting in remarkable detail the life of the townsfolk over three centuries – even the gardens are perfectly in period. Directly opposite, the imposing neo-Gothic Moederkerk was built on the site of the original Dutch Reformed church, which burnt down in 1710. The fascinating Toy and Miniature Museum (Mon–Fri 9am–4.30pm, Sat 9am–2pm; www.stelmus.co.za) occupies an old rectory at the corner of Market and Herte Streets, next to the Tourist Office.

Stellenbosch University Museum (Mon–Sat 9am–4.30pm; www0.sun.ac.za/museum) is home to the University's excellent collection, including displays of tribal artefacts and Maggie Laubser paintings. A more recent addition is the **Rupert Museum** (Mon–Fri 9am–4pm, Sat 9am–noon; www.

⊙ CAPE DUTCH ARCHITECTURE

Unique to South Africa, the Cape Dutch architectural style is essentially an 18th-century adaptation of a classical European building style to African conditions. The genre's distinguishing characteristic, common in older houses all around the Western Cape, though less so in Cape Town than in small towns and rural areas, is an ornate round gable standing tall above the front entrance – a feature derived from medieval houses in Amsterdam. Typical Cape Dutch houses have a steeply pitched thatched roof and whitewashed walls. The oldest houses were built to a U- or T-shaped floor plan, while more ostentatious examples built after the mid-18th century have an H-shaped floor plan.

The classic contours of the Cape Dutch style are well complemented by the shady glades and neat vineyards of the Cape Winelands, which is where the finest examples are found. Particularly worthwhile are the manor houses of the Vergelegen, Boschendal and Groot Constantia Wine Estates, the Old Dutch Reformed church in Franschhoek, and any number of old townhouses lining Stellenbosch's Dorp Street.

Oom Samie se Winkel

rupertmuseum.org), which lies at the western end of Dorp Street overlooking the Eerste River, and displays 350 20th-century South African artworks collected by the late Dr Anton and Huberte Rupert.

Stellenbosch is surrounded by wine farms, but those also within easy day-trip distance of Cape Town include family-friendly **Vergenoegd** (www.vergenoegd.co.za), which offers daily runner duck parades, a restaurant and a Saturday-morning market just off the N2. Arguably the estate most geared to entertaining families is nearby **Spier** (www.spier.co.za), which boasts restaurants and picnic spots, vineyard Segway tours and eagle encounters, artworks and studios, regular summer events and more. Coming from Cape Town along the N2, look out for Cape Town Film Studios just before turning off to these estates, complete with the pirate ship used in the filming of the series Black Sails.

STELLENBOSCH TO FRANSCHHOEK

Franschhoek

Franschhoek ⑩, set in a valley with mountains on three sides, is the culinary showpiece of the Western Cape. With dozens of restaurants offering everything from Cape Malay to Provençal cuisine, it has become a popular place for fashionable Capetonians to wine and dine.

This pretty village was founded in 1688 by Huguenots who came over from France; its name means 'French corner' in Dutch. Their story is told in detail at the **Huguenot Memorial Museum** (Mon–Sat 9am–5pm, Sun 2–5pm; www.museum.co.za), which lies on Lambrecht Street alongside the **Huguenot Monument**, paying tribute to these French settlers.

A number of vineyards can be reached on foot, on a **Franschhoek Cycles** (www.franschhoekcycles.co.za) bicycle or guided tour, or on the popular **Franschhoek Wine Tram** (www.winetram.co.za).

Paarl

The R45 leads northwest from Franschhoek to **Paarl**, the largest Winelands town. En route, **Babylonstoren** (www.babylonstoren.com) wine estate is a recommended detour from the main road for its sprawling Cape Dutch garden a rustic setting for the tasting room, farm shop, café and restaurant. Paarl itself is home to the viticultural giant **KWV** (www.kwv.co.za), once a co-operative. Its 22-hectare (54-acre) cellar complex is one of the world's largest, featuring the awe-inspiring Cathedral Cellar, with a barrel-vaulted roof.

Paarl is rather industrialised and has lost its charm, but has two main claims to historical significance. Here, in 1875, the Afrikaans language was first officially recognised, a fact

Cape Dutch manor house, Boschendal

commemorated by the **Afrikaans Taal Museum** (www.taalmuseum.co.za) on Pastorie Street and, more impressively, the **Taal Monument**. Visiting the latter gives a look at the pearl-like granite outcrop, one of the world's largest, that inspired the town's name. Paarl is also the closest town to **Drakenstein Correctional Centre**, formerly Victor Verster Prison, where Nelson Mandela spent the final years of his 27-year incarceration.

Vineyards near Paarl include **Fairview** (www.fairview.co.za), with its herd of Saanen goats which live in a tall stone tower, and neighbouring **Spice Route** (www.spiceroute.co.za).

Situated a short distance off the R101, the 7½-hectare (18½-acre) **Drakenstein Lion Park** (daily 9.30am–5pm; www.lionrescue.org.za) is home to 15 lions that were born in captivity and cannot be introduced to the wild. Nearby, **Butterfly World** (daily 9am–5pm) is South Africa's largest butterfly park, with more than 20 indigenous species in an attractive landscaped indoor garden, as well as a mesmerising selection of creepy spiders.

HERMANUS AND THE OVERBERG

The best land-based whale-watching in the world is to be found around **Hermanus**, a couple of hours' drive southeast of Cape Town. A day trip to this seaside resort can be immensely rewarding, with cliff viewpoints as little as 30m (98ft) away from these spectacular mammals. The excitement is almost tangible; reports of sightings draw crowds to the shore to watch in wonder. Hermanus can become very crowded, but there are plenty of excellent viewing

⊙ HELSHOOGTE PASS

The R310 northeast from Stellenbosch towards Franschhoek takes you over the stunning Helshoogte Pass, with some of the most beautiful scenery and prestigious estates in the Winelands en route. Head up to the 'vineyard in the sky', **Delaire Graff** (www.delaire.co.za), owned by British diamond magnate Laurence Graff, to see the original of world's most reproduced (and kitschy) painting, *Chinese Girl* (1952) by Russian-Capetonian Vladimir Tretchikoff (1913–2006). From here, the view of the Simonsberg Mountain and across the Franschhoek Valley is memorable, particularly at sunset. Across the road, **Tokora** (www.tokara.com) also offers superb wines, views and art, plus an excellent deli-restaurant. **Boschendal** (www.boschendal.com), on the other side of the Pass, just before the junction with the R45, combines excellent wines and gourmet picnics with a magnificent Cape Dutch manor, furnished in spectacular 17th- and 18th-century style, as well as a paradisiacal garden and mountain-biking trails. Between here and Franschhoek, **Frakschhoek Motor Museum** (www.fmm.co.za) exhibits local billionaire Johann Rupert's vintage car collection and wine estate **La Motte** (www.la-motte.com), also owned by the Ruperts, has a collection of Pierneef paintings, a gourmet restaurant and a hiking trail.

spots from Clarence Drive (east of Gordon's Bay) all the way to the De Hoop Nature Reserve. When it is not whale season, this Overberg ('over the mountain' from Cape Town) region is still well worth visiting, as it combines many of the best aspects of the Western Cape in one relatively compact area. If you have more than a day to spare, a tour of this memorable stretch of coastline can be combined with the Garden Route.

Hermanus lies 110km (68 miles) from Cape Town on the shores of **Walker Bay** ⓫. The quickest route from the city is via the N2, over Sir Lowry's Pass, with its stunning views down to False Bay, then via the R43. An even more scenic route follows Clarence Drive (R44) down the east side of False Bay, providing views to match Chapman's Peak Drive.

A short detour from the N2, **Vergelegen** (daily 9am–5pm; www.vergelegen.co.za) in Somerset West is one of South Africa's most beautiful wine estates. Situated on the slopes of Helderberg Mountain, Vergelegen, which means 'lying afar', started life as a remote outpost of the Cape Colony in 1685 and was later bought by Willem van der Stel, who founded the historic manor house. The magnificent gardens, architecture and museums are complemented by its Stables restaurant and award-winning wines. Neighbouring Lourensford wine estate also makes a pleasant stop.

At Betty's Bay, the renowned **Harold Porter National Botanical Garden** ⓬ (daily 8am–4.30pm; www.sanbi.org) has a network of footpaths and more than 1,600 species of fynbos, showcasing the biodiversity of the surrounding Kogelberg Biosphere Reserve. The wildlife includes baboons and elusive leopards, but the Kogelberg ecosystem was devastated by a manmade fire that began in Betty's Bay and spread east in January 2019. Nearby **Stoney Point Nature Reserve** (daily

8am–4.30pm; www.cap-enature.co.za), home to a colony of African penguins, is also excellent for whale watching.

The R320, which forks off the R43 2km (1 mile) before Hermanus, leads to the upmarket vineyards of the Hemel en Arde ('Heaven and Earth') Valley, including Atraxia (www.ataraxiawines.co.za), Whalehaven (www.whalehavenwines.co.za), Hamilton Russell

Huguenot Monument, Franschhoek

(www.hamiltonrussellvineyards.com), Creation (www.creationwines.com) and Bouchard Finlayson (www.bouchard-finlayson.co.za). The Walker Bay wines produced by these estates are among the most respected and expensive in the country.

Originally a fishing and whaling village, Hermanus is now a popular resort, but the whales continue to contribute to the town's finances – through tourism. The **Old Harbour Museum** (Mon–Sat 9am–4.30pm; www.hermanus.co.za) tells the story of the whaling industry, and the mysterious and soothing songs of the whales out at sea are caught by sonar buoy and transmitted live into the museum.

Hermanus is home to the world's only Whale Crier, who strides through the streets, announcing whale sightings on his unique kelp horn. A toll-free Whale Hotline (tel: 083 910 1028) keeps would-be watchers updated.

The Tip of Africa

Forty-five km (28 miles) south of Bredasdorp, **Cape Agulhas** ⑬ (www.sanparks.org/parks/agulhas) is the southernmost point of Africa. It is here, and not at the Cape of Good Hope, as is often thought, that the Indian and Atlantic oceans meet. The spot is marked by a cairn a short distance from **Agulhas Lighthouse**, which has a café. Unlike the Cape of Good Hope with its dramatic cliffs, the coast at Agulhas slopes gently into the ocean – next stop, Antarctica. Neighbouring Struisbaai boasts an immaculate 14km (8-mile) beach, the longest

⊘ GENTLE GIANTS

From roughly July to December, the waters around the Western Cape host some rare visitors – migrating whales – which breed and calve in sheltered bays along the coastline.

For several months, whale calves can be seen swimming and playing with their mothers. This joyous display is truly unforgettable. Peak viewing time is September to November, and Hermanus holds an annual Whale Festival to celebrate these gentle giants.

Humpback and Bryde's whales can be spotted, but the most common sightings are of southern right whales. With tragic irony, the ages-old, instinctive breeding journey of these magnificent mammals nearly brought about their extinction. Southern right whales were so named because they were the 'right' quarry for whalers. Every bit of these slow-moving mammals could be used, and conveniently, they floated when dead, making retrieval of the bodies easy. Over 12,000 were killed in these waters. Now protected, the population is increasing at a rate of 7 percent per year.

uninterrupted stretch of white sand in Southern Africa.

East of Cape Agulhas lies the idyllic village of **Arniston**, named after a ship wrecked here in 1815. Locals call it Waenhuiskrans, after an enormous cavern eroded into the cliffs close to the village. The undulating Overberg landscape and coastline here are simply stunning. Near the harbour, historic thatched

Whale and calf

fishermen's cottages look over a turquoise sea with rolling white sand dunes in the distance.

Protecting the largest surviving tract of coastal fynbos, the unforgettable **De Hoop Nature Reserve** ⑭ (daily 7am–6pm; www.capenature.co.za) lies about 15km (9 miles) up the coast from Arniston, but it is reached by returning inland to Bredasdorp, then taking a well-marked dirt road. A rich variety of wildlife is associated with the profuse fynbos (1,500 species), including bontebok, Cape mountain zebra, and over 250 bird species, including a rare breeding colony of Cape vultures. Famous for the 55km (34-mile), five-night Whale Trail, the reserve has 50km (31 miles) of spectacular coastline, flanked by pristine white sand dunes rising as high as 90m (295ft). This stretch of water is the breeding ground for most of the Cape's whales. There are upmarket cottages (www.dehoopcollection. com) if you want to stay overnight.

The Lighthouse at Cape Agulhas

THE GARDEN ROUTE

With the exception of Cape Town, the Garden Route is the best-known tourist destination in the Western Cape. Though its name conjures up visions of floral splendour, it is more forest than garden. The title 'Garden Route' reflects the thick vegetation covering the rolling hills lying between the dramatic Outeniqua, Langkloof and Tsitsikamma ranges and the breathtaking shoreline of the Indian Ocean, home to whales and dolphins.

This is a popular resort area for South African holidaymakers and can become very congested during their main Christmas holiday season. Developments catering to tourists have encroached on some of the natural beauty, while a major bush fire decimated the outskirts of Knysna in 2017. However, there is still much to enjoy among these forests, mountains and lagoons.

The Garden Route begins at Mossel Bay, some 400km (248 miles) east of Cape Town, and ends at Storms River, about 190km (118 miles) further east. This is covered by the excellent N2, but to properly experience the area's natural wealth, detour off the main road and take in some of the picturesque older roads through attractive coastal towns and past exquisite lakes, lagoons and rivers.

You can reach Knysna on a lengthy day trip from Cape Town, but this will not allow you time to see very much. It is advisable to allow at least two days, with an overnight stop, to really enjoy the scenery and rustic towns along the way.

Mossel Bay to Wilderness

When you see the industrial approach to **Mossel Bay** ⑮, don't be put off. The centre of the town is charming. Leave plenty of time for the **Bartolomeu Dias Museum Complex** (Mon–Fri 9am–4.45pm, Sat–Sun 9am–3.45pm; www.diasmuseum. co.za), which covers Mossel Bay's role as an early stop-off for European mariners. In its grounds you'll find the 500-year-old Post Office Tree, where sailors used to leave letters for each other; a life-size replica of Bartolomeu Dias's caravel; a maritime museum; a Dutch East India Company granary; an ethno-botanical garden; and a shell museum displaying sea-shells from around the world, as well as a 476kg stuffed great white shark.

The swimming from Santos Beach is among the best on the Garden Route. A cruise around Seal Island with **Ramonza** (www. romonzaboattrips.co.za) will allow you to spot comical African penguins and Cape fur seals, as well as southern right whales and perhaps a humpback.

Some 18km (11 miles) past George, the Garden Route's main town, the N2 bisects **Wilderness** ⑯. Lavish holiday homes now sprawl along the dunes bordering the famed long beach of what was once a small, romantic village.

The village of Wilderness marks the start of the Wilderness section of the **Garden Route National Park** (open daily; www. sanparks.org). This wetland area with its lush forests covers over 2,500 hectares (6,177 acres), stretching 28km (171/2 miles) along the coastline to Sedgefield, and incorporating 15km (just over 9 miles) of inland waterways including five rivers and five lakes. It is the natural habitat for 250 species of birds, including 79 different types of water birds. There are a number of marked hiking trails, and it is also possible to explore the area from the water in rented canoes.

Just after Sedgefield and its large Saturday-morning farmers' market (www.wildoatsmarket.co.za), a right turn towards Buffel's Bay leads to the glorious, undeveloped beach bordering the **Goukamma Nature Reserve** ⑰ (open daily; www.capenature.co.za). The beach is virtually deserted, bathers preferring the more sheltered waters of Buffel's Bay itself, just 1km (0.6 miles) further on. Goukamma covers over 200 sq km (124 square miles), including Groenvlei, a freshwater lake popular with anglers (permits cost R45). Rich wildlife includes fish eagles, rare African black oystercatchers, vervet monkeys, otters and mongoose. Marine life is equally plentiful; dolphins are often seen. During the breeding season (August–November), southern right whales pass by on their migration route.

Little Karoo

Oudtshoorn, the principal town of the Little Karoo, is an interesting side trip from the Garden Route; it's just 63km (39 miles) north of George via the Outeniqua Pass or 85km (53 miles) north of Mossel Bay via the Robinson Pass. Famous for ostrich farming, the region's dry climate makes it ideal for breeding these large, flightless birds, and their favourite food, lucerne (alfalfa), grows well here. It is impossible to travel around the region without seeing flocks of them.

The story of this industry, which enjoyed a glorious heyday from the 1880s until World War I, is chronicled at the excellent **C.P. Nel Museum** (Mon–Fri 8am–5pm, Sat 9am–1pm; www.cpnelmuseum.co.za) on Baron van Rheede Street.

Many ostrich farms are open to the public. You can see the birds hatch, hold the chicks, watch the adults being plucked, eat ostrich meat and buy ostrich-skin products.

North of town is the **Cango Ostrich Farm** (daily 8am–4.30pm; www.cangoostrich.co.za), but first you will pass the **Cango Wildlife Ranch ⑱** (daily 8.30am–4.30pm; www.cango.co.za), 3km (2 miles) out of town. This breeding centre for rare animals and endangered species is a fantastic place to see African wildlife, including cheetahs, crocodiles, snakes and lemurs. It is an unforgettable experience to encounter playful young cheetahs, there as part of the Cheetah Preservation Foundation, or go crocodile cage diving.

Knysna

Knysna ⑲, 102km (63 miles) east of Mossel Bay, and a six-hour drive along the N2 from Cape Town, is situated in an attractive hilly setting on the shores of the tidal Knysna Lagoon. It is one of the main tourist destinations along the Garden Route, and a convenient place to stay, though it has lost some of its charm in the scramble to cash in on tourism. There are, however, no beaches; the Heads (two steep sandstone cliffs) and a coral reef guard the

The Garden Route

Ostrich farm, Oudtshoorn

sea mouth of the lagoon. A cruise to the Heads from Knysna Quay with the likes of the Featherbed Company (www.knysnafeatherbed.com) is a popular excursion, with ferry tickets available from Knysna Tourism (www.visitknysna.co.za) on Main Street. You can also explore the lagoon by kayak or stand-up paddleboard (SUP).

The history of the town, which grew to prosperity on the timber trade that nearly destroyed its massive hardwood forests, is told at the **Knysna Museum** (Mon–Fri 9.30am–4pm, Sat 9.30am–1pm; donations accepted) on Main Street.

To experience the **Diepwalle Forest** ⑳, (open daily; www.sanparks.org), take the R339, a well-maintained unpaved road. Though a shadow of its former self, the forest is still impressive. If you're lucky, you will glimpse a brilliant red-and-green Knysna loerie among the huge, centuries-old stinkwood and yellowwood trees that form a thick canopy overhead. There are three marked Elephant Trails, following the paths of bygone woodcutters. Unfortunately the elephants are no longer here – the few remaining wild pachyderms were relocated to the Shamwari Game Reserve, near Port Elizabeth.

It is possible to buy finely crafted items, made from local hardwoods, from the street markets and craft shops along Main Street, and at the roadside stalls on the N2.

Knysna is lively at night, and has many good restaurants. Look out for beer and oysters: Knysna is home to South Africa's oldest craft brewery, Mitchell's (www.mitchellsbrewing.com), and has a history of oyster farming, although the industry is shifting to the West Coast. Oyster tours (www.knysnacharters.com) are available.

Plettenberg Bay and Tsitsikamma

Thirty km (18 miles) east lies **Plettenberg Bay ㉑**, a beautiful spot spoilt only by the hideous modern hotel built near the beach. It is a fashionable resort with safe bathing, and consequently gets very crowded in high summer. At the south of the bay, the scenic Robberg Peninsula, where you can see seals, dolphins and whales, is protected in the **Robberg Nature Reserve** (8am–5pm; www.capenature.co.za). A round walk to the furthest end of the peninsula takes about four hours.

A large number of dolphins make 'Plett' their home year-round. Boat trips around the bay run from the beach, and Ocean Blue Adventures (tel: 083-701 3583; www.oceanadventures.co.za) offers an informative excursion. The experience of being in a small boat with dolphins playing in the waves, so close that you could

◎ ROUTE 62: TOP TIP

For a break from the N2, follow Route 62 (www.route62. co.za), which claims to be the world's longest wine route, back to Cape Town from the Garden Route. It leads west from Oudtshoorn through the Little Karoo, passing the pretty little farming towns of Calitzdorp, Ladismith, Barrydale and Montagu, before squeezing through the dramatic Cogmanskloof pass in the wrinkly Langeberg range and popping out in the Robertson Wine Valley (www.robertsonwinevalley.com).

Cango Caves

touch them, is incredible. Between August and November there is also a good chance of seeing whales, and you can get updates on their presence from the Tourism Bureau (tel: 044-533 4065, www. plett-tourism.co.za) on Main Street.

The strikingly beautiful Tsitsikamma section of the **Garden Route National Park** (gates open 7am–7pm; www.sanparks.org) encompasses hardwood forests, sparkling pools, coral reefs, dunes, long stretches of sandy beach with swimming spots, deep gorges, waterfalls and the Otter Trail, one of the most popular hikes in the country. One of the world's highest bungee jumps is also here. Those adventurous enough to leap off Bloukrans River Bridge (www.faceadrenalin.com) have a 216m (708ft) fall before they are snapped back up again. The many other adventure activities in the forests and ravines include "kloofing" (canyoning, a mix of swimming, hiking and rappelling) and kayaking.

At **Storms River Mouth**, the main tourist focus within Tsitsikamma, the Garden Route ends in a spectacular fashion. Cliffs covered in dense forest lead down to black rocks against which waves crash violently. You can walk along the boardwalk from the restaurant at Storms River Mouth Rest Camp and gaze down at the surging waters of the river mouth from the 77m-long suspension bridge. Nearby Storms River (a forest hamlet) makes a great base.

THE WEST COAST AND CEDERBERG

The 400km (248-mile) stretch of land north of Cape Town that forms the West Coast is an area of diverse beauty. It lacks the lushness of the Garden Route or the Winelands, but its attractions are considerable. The Atlantic Ocean bestows on this region a wild coastline, a rich harvest of seafood, huge and varied communities of seabirds, and the awe-inspiring spectacle of migrating whales. Inland, the rugged Cederberg Mountains form its eastern border, their fascinating rock formations attracting hikers and climbers. Ancient rock paintings speak of human life

⊙ LIGHTS, CAMERA, CAPE TOWN!

Cape Town has become popular in the last decade as an affordable destination for shooting both series and big-budget movies: *Blood Diamond*, *Invictus*, *Rendition*, *Safe House* and *Judge Dredd*, to name just a few. At **Cape Town Film Studios** (www.capetownfilmstudios.co.za), the first state-of-the art facility of its kind in Sub-Saharan Africa, you can see the pirate ship left from the series *Black Sails* from the N2 highway. As *Homeland* season four demonstrated, Cape Town's diverse scenery appeals to production companies (the city stood in for Islamabad, Pakistan).

here long before the arrival of the first Europeans, and a wealth of wildlife can be seen. Between mountains and ocean lie the wheat fields and vineyards of the Swartland, and wildflowers carpet the whole region in a vibrant springtime display.

On a day-long excursion from Cape Town, you can travel along the R27, visiting the town of Darling and the West Coast National Park. Alternatively, you could spend a night or two in the Cederberg Wilderness Area and view ancient rock paintings and remarkable natural sandstone sculptures. A two- to three-day excursion would accommodate a loop right around the region.

Not far from central Cape Town on the R27 is the suburb of **Bloubergstrand** ("Blue Mountain Beach"), with its unrivalled view of Table Mountain, seen across Table Bay. The small town of **Darling** lies further along the R27, 70km (43 miles) north of Cape Town, avoiding Atlantis for safety reasons. Among Darling's attractions are a small wine route, including **Groote Post** (www.grootepost.com), and the **Evita se Perron** (www. evita.co.za) cabaret by Evita Bezuidenhout (aka Pieter-Dirk Uys), South Africa's answer to Dame Edna Everage. The annual spring flower show, held annually since 1917, is a major event.

The wetlands of the **West Coast National Park** ㉒ (daily 7am–7pm; www.sanparks. org) attract millions of marine birds, including waders, pelicans, black oystercatchers and flamingos, to the shores and islands of the saltwater **Langebaan Lagoon**. On a peninsula west of the lagoon, the **Postberg Nature Reserve** is one of the closest areas

Eve's Footprints

A set of fossilised footprints discovered in West Coast National Park in 1995 dates back 120,000 years, the oldest footprints of anatomically modern human beings known from anywhere in the world.

to Cape Town for viewing spring wildflowers, and it protects wildlife such as oryx and springbok, but is only open for a few weeks during the wildflower season of August and September (7am–7pm; tel: 022-772 2144 for opening times; www.sanparks. org). Geelbek Information Centre has replicas of Eve's Footprints, which were discovered by the lagoon in 1995.

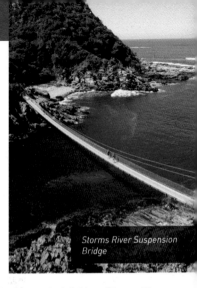
Storms River Suspension Bridge

Further along the R27 lies **Paternoster**, a beautiful whitewashed fishing village with colourful boats on its long beach and good seafood restaurants that attract weekending Capetonians.

Two hours north of Paternoster, the fishing port of **Lambert's Bay** is dominated by the huge colonies of seabirds 100m (328ft) offshore at **Bird Island ㉓** (daily 7am–6pm; tel: 027-432 1672; www.lambertsbay.co.za). You can walk out along a breakwater to the island, where masses of noisy blue-eyed Cape gannets, cormorants and African penguins can be seen from a special viewing tower. Boat trips operate from Lambert's Bay to view visiting whales (July–November), and you can catch a glimpse of Cape fur seals, penguins and endemic Heaviside's dolphins year-round.

Some 60km (37 miles) east along the R364 is the northern tip of the Cederberg Mountains and the **Cederberg Wilderness Area ㉔** (open daily; www.capenature.org.za). Time and the

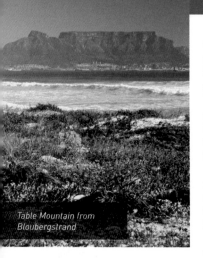
Table Mountain from Bloubergstrand

elements have eroded the sandstone into a surreal landscape that stretches as far as the eye can see. The most extraordinary shapes are reached along hiking trails in the south of the reserve. They include the **Wolfberg Arch**, a 15m- (49ft-) high natural rock archway reached via the Wolfberg Cracks, and the **Maltese Cross**, a 30m- (98ft-) tall pillar.

Vegetation includes wild olives, purple-blue *ridderspoor*, the rare snow protea, and rooibos (see page 106). The region is named after the Clanwilliam cedar tree, which grows against cliffs, overhanging at altitudes of more than 1000m (3,280ft) above sea level. Wildlife includes baboons, porcupine, aardvark, caracal, Cape fox, mongoose and leopard. Puff adders and black spitting cobras inhabit the undergrowth, and Clanwilliam yellowfish swim in the Olifants River, named after the great herds of elephants that once roamed on the vast plains to the south of the mountains.

This region was a favourite hunting ground of San (Bushmen) for thousands of years. Their **rock paintings** remain throughout the area, including the beautiful private wilderness areas of Bushmans Kloof and Kagga Kamma (see page 142), where guided walks reveal what is known of their history. The craggy scenery features rock art dating back an incredible 6,000 years, and activities incude stargazing, nature drives and mountain biking.

Clanwilliam is a decent base for exploring the area, with accommodation, a good restaurant and, of course, rooibos tea.

Cape Town is about three hours' drive down the N7, past Citrusdal and the Swartland's giant, golden wheat fields. En route, look to the horizon for a long-distance view of Table Mountain.

⊙ 'FEATHER MILLIONAIRES'

Towards the end of the 19th century, the demand for ostrich plumes for the hats and feather boas of the ladies of fashion was unprecedented. Prices soared as ostrich feathers became a commodity of enormous value, and, as a consequence, many ostrich farmers around Oudtshoorn became millionaires.

These 'feather barons' threw themselves enthusiastically into the extravagant lifestyle their newfound wealth bought them. Their excesses rivalled those of the Randlords of Johannesburg, who made countless millions from gold and diamonds.

They built themselves elaborate sandstone mansions, known as 'feather palaces', splendid examples of which can be seen in Oudtshoorn today. Many of these were an unfortunate combination of lavish spending and question-able taste. The well-preserved **Le Roux Townhouse**, on the corner of Loop and High Streets, is one of the greatest of these mansions. Visitors to the **Safari Ostrich Farm** (www. safariostrich), a working ostrich farm 6km south of town on the R328, can visit Welgeluk, another feather palace.

When ostrich feathers fell out of fashion at the start of World War I, the market crashed spectacularly, reducing many of the feather millionaires to poverty.

Green Point Market

WHAT TO DO

SHOPPING

Arts and crafts from all over Africa can be bought in Cape Town's markets and shops. If you want a uniquely South African souvenir, look out for Zulu pottery, basketry and beadwork; ostrich products, such as egg lamps; colourful textiles; and township art. These vary in quality, but it is not difficult to find beautifully made items and highly original souvenirs at relatively low cost. Traditional West and Central African carved wooden masks, made to celebrate events such as a birth or wedding, also make a fascinating souvenir. Other African objects to look out for include soapstone carvings, intricate beadwork, colourful fabrics, basketwork and wooden bowls.

Gold, diamonds and other gems, both precious and semi-precious, are readily available, with many talented jewellery designers working in the region. Cape Town's V&A Waterfront has the fun Scratch Patch (see page 40), numerous jewellers and the Cape Town Diamond Museum (www.capetowndiamondmuseum.org) with a well-stocked shop.

Colonial antiques, including porcelain, glassware, furniture and jewellery, are also much in evidence, as are contemporary art, leather goods and ceramics. Keep an eye out for colourful Ardmore Ceramics (http://ardmoreceramics.co.za) – animal-themed ceramics crafted by Zulu artisans in the Drakensburg that have even been shown at Christie's in London (a large portion of the funds from the sale of Ardmore ceramics go towards AIDS education). A Cape equivalent is Zizamele (www.zizamele.co.za), which has a stall in the Watershed (see page

38). You will also see brightly painted ostrich eggs, and bags, wallets, belts and shoes made from ostrich skin.

Few travellers return home without at least one bottle of the fine wine for which the region is renowned, and tasting before you buy is all part of the fun. Most reputable vineyards and wine shops can arrange to ship sizeable purchases to your home. There is also a limited but representative selection in Big Five Duty Free at Cape Town airport.

WHERE TO SHOP

Cape Town and its suburbs are dotted with an ever-increasing selection of malls, where a wide variety of chain and boutique stores are clustered under one roof. The best pick for visitors is the sprawling Victoria Wharf Shopping Mall, at the conveniently located V&A Waterfront (see page 38). The main chain stores are represented here, while souvenir and craft shops tend to be dotted between the Waterfront's outdoor bars and cafés. The Watershed is a fantastic source of high-quality items, with over 150 stalls filling a converted warehouse with ceramics, township art, shweshwe fabric toys and everything in between.

Other popular malls include Canal Walk (https://canalwalk. co.za), northeast of the city centre, the Gardens Centre (www. gardensshoppingcentre.co.za), Cape Quarter (www.capequarter.co.za) in fashionable De Waterkant, Cavendish Square (www.cavendish.co.za) in Claremont, Blue Route (www.blueroutemall.co.za) in Tokai and Long Beach (www.longbeachmall. co.za) near Noordhoek.

The nearby Streetwires (www.streetwires.co.za) social upliftment project was founded in 2000 with the aim of employing as many wire workers as possible; the craftspeople here can make anything from beaded toys and bowls to wine racks and gorgeous wire chandeliers.

Markets sell African arts and crafts for lower prices than shops, although stores in the likes of the Cape Quarter offer a curated selection and more relaxed browsing. Brightly coloured African fabrics, handcrafted clothes and more abound Greenmarket Square, while nearby St George's Mall is lined with dozens of craft stalls and clothing and jewellery shops. Many items sold here are not from Southern African, though you'll be told otherwise; they are largely from West Africa, and sold by Nigerians who have come to Cape Town to make a buck. Nearby Long Street is a particularly good source of antique clothing and secondhand books; check out the 65-year-old Clarke's Bookshop (www.clarkesbooks.co.za). The Pan-African Market, sprawling across three crammed storeys at 76 Long Street, has imported craft-work from all over Africa, along with local craftsmen, musicians, tailors and hairbraiders, and a café serving local staples.

The market at Kirstenbosch National Botanical Garden (last Sunday of every month, September–May) is notable for the quality crafts on offer. In the charming small towns along the Cape Peninsula you will find lots of local crafts and art, often of a very high standard, some sold from roadside stalls. Kalk Bay, Hout Bay and Noordhoek are known for their artists, sculptors and potters, while the Mariner's Wharf at Hout Bay boasts a

Greenmarket Square

shop specialising in maritime memorabilia, including shipwreck relics. Hout Bay also has a popular weekend market (www.bayharbour.co.za) and historic Simon's Town is well-endowed with antique shops. Kalk Bay is arguably one of the best places to shop on the Cape, with a string of art and antique shops along the main drag. You can also buy fresh fish straight off the boat as fishermen dock in the harbour with their catch of the day.

ENTERTAINMENT

Cape Town has a cosmopolitan cultural milieu, with some excellent theatre and live music on offer, as well as one of Africa's most vibrant party scenes. The daily and weekly newspapers contain events listings and guides to what's on, while local radio station Good Hope FM 96.7 is another good source of information, as are the Mail & Guardian website, www.mg.co.za, and Cape Town Magazine (www.capetownmagazine.co.za).

THEATRE AND LIVE MUSIC

The premier venue for performing arts is the Artscape Complex (www.artscape.co.za) in the Foreshore section of the city centre. With three auditoriums, this concrete complex is home to the Cape Town Philharmonic Orchestra, Cape Town Opera and Jazzart modern dance company, and hosts a busy programme of classical music, ballet, opera, drama, light musicals and cabaret performances.

The Baxter Theatre (www.baxter.co.za) in Rondebosch presents contemporary music, theatre, comedy and more. If your taste is more traditional, Shakespeare's plays can be seen in a romantic outdoor setting under the night sky at the Maynardville Open-Air Theatre (www.maynardville.co.za) in Wynberg, during January and February. Of the numerous smaller independent theatres, Alexander Bar, Café & Theatre (www.alexanderbar.co.za), above a bar in the city centre, and the Fugard Theatre (www.thefugard.com) in the East City are popular. Oude Libertas Amphitheatre (http://oudelibertas. co.za) in Stellenbosch stages outdoor music and theatre performances among the grapevines from November to March, while many wine estates offer summer events under the stars.

Live music can be heard at all the city's theatres, including classical, jazz and rock, as well as traditional and

⊘ GUIDES AND TOURS

Innumerable tour companies operate in the region, offering everything from walking tours of the historic city centre to trips along the Garden Route lasting over a week. The two most popular day trips take in Cape Point and the Winelands, while Bo-Kaap 'cooking safaris' and shark-cage diving out of Simon's Town and Gansbaai are also popular. All tour guides speak English, and some also speak French, German or Spanish. Certain areas, such as the Cape Flats, should only be visited as part of a tour party, while only official tours are allowed to land on Robben Island.

Kirstenbosch

contemporary variations on African music. Try to take in one of the summer Sunday outdoor performances at the Kirstenbosch National Botanical Garden, and enjoy picnicking and listening to music in beautiful surroundings. Other venues include the Amphitheatre at the V&A Waterfront, which regularly puts on free concerts, and the Waiting Room (www.facebook.com/WaitingRoomCT) on Long Street for DJs and bands.

Cape Town is known for its distinctive jazz, influenced by traditional African music and made most famous by Abdullah Ibrahim (previously known as 'Dollar Brand'). Central venues include The Crypt Jazz Restaurant (www.thecryptjazz.com), located beneath St George's Cathedral, and The Piano Bar (www.thepianobar.co.za) in De Waterkant, although aficionados may prefer a jazz-themed township tour with the likes of Coffeebeans Routes (www.coffeebeansroutes.com). And then, of course, there is the Cape Town International Jazz Festival (www.capetownjazzfest.

com), Africa's largest jazz festival, which draws acts from across the globe to the city over the last weekend in March.

NIGHTLIFE

Welcome to party town! Cape Town is known for its varied and vibrant nightlife, ranging from raucous pubs and hipster bars to chichi clubs and LGBTQ hangouts. Nightclubs typically stay open until between 2am and 4am, seven nights a week in some cases. A safe and popular area is The V&A Waterfront, which has plenty of bars and restaurants, but can be quiet after dark. Long, Bree and the surrounding streets in the city centre attract the young and hip, who spend all night wandering between the enormous selection of pubs and clubs.

Somerset Road and the surrounding areas of De Waterkant and Green Point are the main focal point hub of the gay scene; don't miss a burger and a show at Beefcakes (www.beefcakes.co.za).

SPORTS

South Africans are mad about sports, both as spectators and participants, and Cape Town's moderate climate means that many activities can be enjoyed year-round. The geography of the region is perfect for all kinds of outdoor pursuits, including swimming, watersports, horse-riding, cycling, golf, hiking, climbing and paragliding.

SPECTATOR SPORTS

The rugby and cricket stadia in Newlands, overlooked by the eastern slopes of Table Mountain, regularly host key provincial and international fixtures. Rugby and cricketing standards are very high. The South African national side, the Springboks, has won the Rugby World Cup twice (1995 and 2007), and the Proteas national cricket team is also considered to be one of the world's finest, with several of its players hailing from the Western Cape.

South Africa hosted the Rugby and Cricket World Cups in 1995 and 2003 and followed this up by hosting the 2010 FIFA Football World Cup, making it the first country after the UK to achieve this prestigious sporting hat trick. While Spain took home the prize for the 2010 World Cup, the event put Cape Town on the international map with football fans the world over visiting South Africa in droves and the city playing prominently in the media during the games.

The city's leading football side, Ajax Cape Town, competes in the South African Premium League during the southern winter. It plays at Cape Town Stadium and Athlone Stadium on the Cape Flats; see www.psl.co.za for fixtures. Several talented players started their career here before making their name in the English Premiership, notably Benni McCarthy, Steven Pienaar and Quinton Fortune. Details of forthcoming rugby, football and cricket fixtures can be found in the local press.

Horse-racing is another popular spectator sport. There are racetracks at Durbanville, Kenilworth and Milnerton, and racehorses bred in the Robertson Valley. The Sun Met (www.sunmet.co.za), held each January at Kenilworth

Sunset in Camps Bay

(www.krca.co.za), is a highly prestigious sporting and social event, where the fashions worn by racegoers are almost as important as what is happening on the track.

Every March, Cape Town plays host to the famous Cape Town Cycle Tour (http://capetowncycletour.com), previously known as the Cape Argus. Over 30,000 competitors, including many from overseas, race along a stunning 109km (65-mile) route around the Cape Peninsula. The sheer number of riders, plus the lavish costumes some wear, makes this a spectacular event to watch.

The city forms part of the route for many running marathons, the most important being the Cape Peninsula Marathon (February) and the 56km (35-mile) Two Oceans Marathon (Easter Saturday; www.twooceansmarathon.org.za), both of which draw competitors from all around the world.

Cape Town is a popular stopping point for round-the-world yacht races. The Cape-to-Rio race (www.cape2rio2020.com) leaves from here, with the next competition planned for 2020, while the city also features in the Volvo Ocean Race (www.volvooceanrace.com).

ACTIVE PURSUITS

Sports enthusiasts are spoilt for choice in Cape Town. Huge amounts of money have been invested in sporting facilities, which are generally excellent.

Golfers can choose between more than a dozen superb courses in glorious locations, including The Royal Cape at Wynberg (www.royalcapegolf.co.za), the country's oldest golf club (established 1885), and Milnerton Golf Club (www.milnertongolf.co.za) on Woodbridge Island. Most clubs welcome visitors, charging around R700 for 18 holes.

Horse-riding is another popular activity, with plenty of beautiful places to ride, including beaches and vineyards; try Sleepy Hollow

International rugby at Newlands

Horse Riding (www.sleepy-hollowhorseriding.co.za) in Noordhoek. Mountain-biking is also popular in the Cape's mountains, either independently or with the likes of Day Trippers (www.daytrippers.co.za). If you prefer to exercise on your own two feet, there are innumerable hiking trails throughout the national parks and reserves, and many hikers head for Table Mountain at weekends. Again, guided tours are available, and are a good way to get your bearings in the bush.

With so much coastline, it is not surprising that watersports-lovers are well catered for. Some of the best surfers in the world make their home in South Africa, and there are surfing competitions at Kommetjie, while windsurfing, kitesurfing and stand-up paddleboarding are popular in spots such as Langebaan Lagoon. Scuba diving among the shipwrecks and kelp forests is a fascinating way to study the ecosystem off the Cape. False Bay's sevengill sharks are thought to live for up to 400 years, and Gansbaai (near Hermanus) is famous for cage diving to see great whites. Not all the beaches are suitable for swimming, either due to treacherous currents and pounding surf or because the water is too cold, but there are plenty of places where it is safe to swim (see page 95).

The same combination of the warm Indian Ocean and cooler Atlantic that makes the waters so alluring to divers is responsible for the remarkable wealth of marine life that brings fishermen in their droves. Standing, fishing rod in hand, on a virtually deserted beach, with golden-white sand stretching as far as the eye can see, is an idyllic experience few forget. Deep-sea game fishermen can charter boats and there are fly-fishing opportunities in areas such as the Overberg and Breede River Valley, although other parts of the country are better for fly-fishing.

Those with a sense of adventure can enjoy white-water rafting along the Breede or Palmiet river, climb Table Mountain, paraglide off Lion's Head or zip-line through the Hottentots Holland Mountains (www.canopytour.co.za). If a more serene form of outdoor activity appeals, hot-air ballooning over the Winelands or whale-watching in Hermanus is probably the answer.

BEACHES

Cape Town's coastal suburbs boast unrivalled beaches, with great stretches of clean, golden sand, some miles long, with the ocean on one side and majestic mountains on the other. Whether your preference is for sheltered coves or wild expanses of unspoilt dunes, for dozing in the sunshine or tackling breaking waves on a surfboard, you will find a beach to suit you.

The beaches on the rugged Atlantic coast, which runs down the western side of the peninsula, while perfect for walking and sunbathing, aren't ideal for swimming, unless you're very hardy. The water temperature is chilly, seldom rising above 15°C (59°F). Those on the False Bay seaboard, north and east of Cape Point, have warmer waters, though they can get overcrowded. The wind off the ocean can be a problem, whipping up the fine sand into a stinging cloud, and the False Bay beaches are battered in summer by vicious southeasterly winds.

On the Atlantic coast, the closest beaches to the city centre are at Sea Point. The sea here is unsuitable for swimming and

Whale-watching tour in Hermanus

the beaches generally rocky, but strolling along the promenade is a Cape Town ritual. A little further south is the very fashionable resort of Clifton, with its expensive yachts and modernist mansions. It has four small beaches, all sandy, sheltered and extremely popular with the young and beautiful. Swimming is safe, but the water painfully cold. Parking is a nightmare (don't even try in the peak summer season), but there are regular buses from the city centre. LGBTQ travellers should check out Clifton Third; if in doubt, head to Fourth.

Camps Bay, a mile or so south of Clifton, is another fashionable residential suburb, with fantastic views of Lion's Head, the Twelve Apostles mountains and the Atlantic Ocean. The broad beach attracts families, and the lively seafront strip has both upmarket and affordable restaurants and cafés.

The stunning beach at Llandudno, 20km (12 miles) south of central Cape Town, is a fabulous, sheltered cove set at the foot of a mountain, with giant boulders dominating the landscape. Sunsets are memorable and the sunbathing idyllic, but the surf is dangerous. A 20-minute walk from Llandudno is Sandy Bay, the main nudist beach for Cape Town. Accessible only by walking along a path through the fynbos and over rocks, it is an exceptionally pretty and relatively sheltered spot, although nude sunbathing can be a painful experience when the wind off the ocean blows the sand around.

Noordhoek's Long Beach, at the end of the thrilling journey along Chapman's Peak Drive, is incredibly impressive, with smooth white sand stretching for over 6km (3.7 miles). Swimming can be hazardous off this gloriously wild beach, which is very popular with horse-riders. Stay close to the car park at the northern end, or head to Kommetjie instead, as there have been muggings in the beach's isolated central section.

The water in the small basin at Kommetjie, a 15km (9-mile) drive from Noordhoek, is popular for swimming, the temperature here a little higher than the ocean. Surfers tackle the breakers in this area, which hosts surfing competitions.

The beaches in the Cape of Good Hope Nature Reserve are great for windswept walks, but few are suitable for swimming, though some have safe tidal pools on the more sheltered False Bay side.

Swimming is safe in the cove at Smitswinkelbaai on the False Bay coast, but the beach is accessible only by walking down a vast number of steps. Miller's Point has several sandy beaches and rare wildlife, including black zonure lizards, but 5km (3 miles) north lies one of the most popular areas on the False Bay seaboard, Boulders. As the name implies, this series of small beaches is distinguished by numerous massive rocks, but its real claim to fame is the community of endangered African penguins that live in a protected reserve on the beach. The combination of beautiful beach, crystal-clear rock pools, relatively warm water and these wonderful black-and-white birds is irresistible. Don't touch or feed the penguins, which have sharp beaks.

Fish Hoek has a superb family beach, with safe swimming and good facilities, while St James, northeast of Fish Hoek on the M4, is popular with families for its large tidal pool. With its Victorian bathing chalets, Muizenberg's long beach can get overcrowded, but there are plenty of seaside activities such as miniature golf and water slides (www.muizenbergslides.co.za).

The most popular beaches generally have parking lots, but in high season it can be virtually impossible to find space. Those along the False Bay seaboard are well served by trains from Cape Town, as far south as Simon's Town. Don't leave your valuables unattended on the beach; if you are driving, conceal them in your car boot – and do so before you arrive and park.

CHILDREN'S CAPE TOWN

Like all of South Africa, Cape Town and the Western Cape are generally very welcoming to children, and there is plenty to keep the kids entertained. The beaches are a huge family attraction, and older children are thrilled by the cable-car ride to the top of Table Mountain and the chance to spot ostriches and baboons at Cape Point. Older kids and teenagers, who want to understand the recent history of South Africa, should find a trip to Robben Island thought-provoking and moving.

Many of the museums and exhibitions are geared to entertain younger visitors, notably the South African Museum, with its dinosaur section and Whale Well. The adjoining Planetarium offers regular children's shows. In Rondebosch in the Southern Suburbs, the Baxter stages children's theatre. Popular central parks include Blue Train Park (www.thebluetrainpark.co.za)

at Mouille Point, Green Point Park (www.gprra.co.za) and Deer Park Café (www.deerparkcafe.co.za) in Vredehoek.

The V&A Waterfront has lots to offer kids. Kids can scrabble for semi-precious stones at the Scratch Patch on Dock Road, which has another branch in Simon's Town, and literally get to grips with life under the sea in the touch tanks of the Two Oceans Aquarium. The exhibits at the Maritime Centre are also interesting to explore.

Third Beach, Clifton

The penguins at Boulders Beach are popular with children, and even the most blasé teenager cannot help but be impressed by the majestic sight of whales at Hermanus. Other popular animal attractions include Hout Bay's World of Birds, Africa's largest bird park, and, in the Winelands, Butterfly World Zoo (www.butterflyworld.co.za), Giraffe House (www.giraffehouse.co.za) and Drakenstein Lion Park (www.lionrescue.org.za).

SCENIC TRAIN JOURNEYS

A train journey provides an unusual way to see the Cape. Cape Town's local commuter rail operator, Metrorail (www.metrorail.co.za, www.cttrains.co.za), operates one service of interest to tourists. Their southern line runs from Cape Town to Simon's

Town via Muizenberg and Kalk Bay, passing some fine scenery along the False Bay Coast. It might be world's most scenic commuter train, but keep your wits about you and, outside the morning and afternoon rush hours, only travel in a group. Stick to the (nominal) first class carriages and don't take the train after dark. Other services run out east to Stellenbosch and Strand, but these are not considered safe.

Train stations are often not signposted, so you will need a map to help you find them. Tickets should be bought in advance from the station, where timetables are posted. Services are frequent during peak commuting times, but delays are common.

The luxurious Rovos Rail operates journeys from Pretoria to Cape Town or the Victoria Falls and beyond in 1930s carriages (tel: 021-421 4020, www.rovos.co.za). If budget and time are no problem, treat yourself to a trip on the legendary Blue Train, one of the most luxurious trains in the world, between Cape Town and Pretoria (tel: 012-334 8459, www.bluetrain.co.za). Shosholoza Meyl's more affordable Premier Classe (www.premierclasse. co.za) and Tourist Class (www.shosholozameyl.co.za) services also ply this route across the Karoo; book through African Sun Travel (www.southafricanrailways.co.za) or JB Train Tours (www. jbtours.co.za). On Tourist Class trains, solo travellers can buy two tickets to guarantee they get a two-berth coupé to themselves. Visit the Man in Seat 61 (www.seat61.com/SouthAfrica) for more info.

Another more affordable option is one of the epic journeys aboard Shongololo Express (tel: 012-315 8242, www.shongololo.com) which combines cross-country rail travel by night with daytime excursions by minibuses, carried on board the train. The 15-day trip between Cape Town and Pretoria includes some of the top tourist destinations in South Africa, while other activities take in Victoria Falls and Namibia.

CALENDAR OF EVENTS

There are many exciting celebrations and activities happening in and around Cape Town throughout the year. Cape Town Tourism and the various regional tourist boards have full listings (see page 134).

January Kaapse Klopse (Cape Town Minstrel Carnival, 2 January); Cape-to-Rio yacht race, Cape Town; Sun Met, Kenilworth.

February Dias & Port Festival, Mossel Bay; Cape Peninsula Marathon; Cape Town Pride Pageant (city centre); Stellenbosch Wine Festival.

March Cape Town Cycle Tour; Cape Town Festival (music, drama and other arts performances); Cape Town International Jazz Festival; Cape Town Carnival; end of Oude Libertas season, Stellenbosch, and Kirstenbosch Summer Sunset Concerts; Cape Town Fashion Week.

April Two Oceans Marathon, Cape Town (Easter Saturday); Klein Karoo National Arts Festival, Oudtshoorn.

May Franschhoek Literary Festival; Pink Loerie Mardi Gras & Arts Festival, Knysna.

June Encounters South African International Documentary Festival, Cape Town; Calitzdorp Winter Festival; whale-watching begins.

July Franschhoek Bastille Festival; Knysna Oyster Festival; Berg River Canoe Marathon, Paarl; Lipton Challenge Cup yacht race, Cape Town.

August Jive Cape Town Funny Festival, Baxter Theatre Complex; spring wildflower bloom begins; Voorkamerfest Performing Arts Festival, Darling.

September Darling Wild Flower and Orchid Show; Fernkloof Flower Festival, Hermanus; Hermanus Whale Festival; Nederburg Wine Auction, Paarl; Franschhoek Uncorked Festival; False Bay Yacht Club Spring Regatta, Simon's Town; Paternoster Spring Crayfish Festival.

October Rocking the Daisies (music), Darling; Cape Town International Kite Festival, Muizenberg.

November Winelands Marathon, Stellenbosch; start of Oude Libertas and Kirstenbosch Summer Sunset Concerts seasons.

December Christmas Carols, Kirstenbosch gardens; Christmas markets; Cape Town Race Week, Table Bay; Franschhoek Cap Classique and Champagne Festival; Mother City Queer Project, Cape Town.

EATING OUT

Everyone will find something to suit their appetite in Cape Town and the Winelands, where eating well is a big part of the local lifestyle. Drawing on its Mediterranean climate, vineyards and miles of fertile farmland, the city is famed for the quality and range of its cuisine, and it is remarkably easy to eat out well without blowing the holiday budget.

Whether you want a snack in a hip bistro or an elegant candlelit dinner in sumptuous surroundings, you will find it in and around Cape Town. The V&A Waterfront alone is home to a range of eateries to suit all tastes and pockets, while the Southern Suburbs and Winelands towns – Franschhoek in particular – boast many fine restaurants, often in superb old Cape Dutch buildings. Breakfast at a weekend food market has become a Cape Town tradition.

As befits a cosmopolitan city, the cuisine of many countries is available, including Chinese, French, Greek, Italian, Indian, Japanese, Thai and Turkish. Restaurants also offer local dishes and traditional food from other parts of Africa, such as Ethiopia and Morocco.

Picnicking

With the excellent climate and glorious beaches and countryside close at hand, picnics are popular. Many beaches have dedicated picnic areas, and excellent, easily portable food can be bought from delicatessens. Some hotels will prepare picnics for their guests, and the vineyards often sell gourmet picnics, to be enjoyed in their grounds.

WHEN TO EAT

Breakfast is available from coffee shops from about 9am; earlier in the city. It's included in most midrange accommodation, while backpacker places may have a café serving breakfast. Wonderful afternoon teas are served at top hotels, including the Mount Nelson, Twelve Apostles and Cape Grace, while most restaurants offer both lunch and dinner. Starting around 6.30pm, dinner generally runs until about 10pm, though in areas such as the V&A Waterfront restaurants may open later.

Afternoon tea at Mount Nelson

Especially in small towns, it is worth confirming opening times in advance, and remember that not all restaurants open every day. The most popular restaurants can sometimes be fully booked for weeks in advance, so consider booking before you travel. It is often possible to book online.

CAPE MALAY & INDIAN CUISINE

The city's history can be traced through its food. Dutch, English, French, German and Portuguese culinary influences have all played a part, but the most significant is that of the 'Malay' slaves who came from the East Indies in the 17th century.

Local Cape Malay specialities include *bobotie*, a sweetish curried minced lamb served with a topping of baked savoury custard; *sosaties*, a sort of marinated kebab; *bredie*, a spicy stew traditionally made from venison or mutton and often accompanied by a sweetened vegetable or fruit dish; *smoorsnoek*, lightly curried snoek, a local line fish; mild and fragrant curry, eaten with roti and sambal, a tomato-and-onion side dish; samoosas (samosas); and coconut-sprinkled doughy *koeksisters*.

High in the Bo-Kaap neighbourhood, the traditional home of the Cape Muslims (as Cape Malay people are now called), Bo-Kaap Kombuis specialises in Cape Malay cuisine. Otherwise, restaurants specialising in Cape Malay are few and far between, but the dishes appear on many menus, including at Jonkershuis, Lord Nelson Restaurant at the Mount Nelson, Signal Restaurant at the Cape Grace and the V&A Food Market (www.waterfront-foodmarket.com). You will also find them in remixed form at the Company's Garden Restaurant (www.thecompanysgarden.com) and, in Constantia, the Norval Foundation gallery's Skotnes Restaurant and the Greenhouse at the Cellars Hohenort. The best way to try this cuisine is on a Cape Malay 'cooking safari', where you prepare the dishes before eating in a culinary guru's Bo-Kaap home. These fun tours are offered by Cooking with Love (www.facebook.com/Faldela1), Andulela and Coffeebeans Routes.

Another South African favourite is bunny chow: scooped-out half loaves of white bread with mutton, lamb, chicken or bean curry filling. The filling dish originated when Indian migrant workers in KwaZulu-Natal sought a convenient way to carry curry lunches to the sugar cane fields. More common in Durban, bunnys may be found in the Eastern Food Bazaar (www.easternfood-bazaar.co.za) at 96 Longmarket Street in Cape Town's city centre.

STUNNING SEAFOOD

As might be expected of a city surrounded by ocean frontage, Cape Town is renowned for its excellent fresh seafood, which is offered by most of the city's leading restaurants. For inexpensive seafood, there are numerous fish-and-chips shops, such as in Kalk Bay and Hout Bay, and Ocean Basket (www.oceanbasket.com) is a popular chain, represented at the V&A Waterfront among other locations.

*Two Oceans Restaurant,
Cape Point*

At more upmarket eateries, the choice and quality of fresh seafood can be outstanding. Shellfish, including crayfish, lobster, oysters (often served with hot chilli sauce) and mussels, are in plentiful supply, as are the extremely tasty linefish, including snoek, yellowtail, kingklip and kabeljou. Since the Russians decimated the Mozambique prawn beds with over-fishing, prawns have tended to be expensive. The Southern African Sustainable Seafood Initiative (www.wwfsassi.co.za) details which fish are endangered.

South Africans love to braai – barbecue – and seafood lends itself particularly well to this form of cooking. If you are fond of fish, try to make the time to head along the coastal roads to of one of the open-air seafood restaurants, especially Die Strandloper on the beach at Langebaan. Here you get the chance, over a 10-course meal, to taste the freshest seafood on the West Coast, which is the country's fishing capital.

MEAT, MEAT... AND MORE MEAT

Most South Africans are great meat-eaters and the range on offer is impressive. Menus are often supplemented by more unusual varieties, including ostrich and less-recommendable crocodile.

Steak remains one of the most common choices, optionally accompanied by monkey-gland sauce (a sort of chutney) or a more

☉ ROOIBOS TEA

Don't leave Cape Town without trying one of the indigenous specialities – rooibos tea. This remarkably versatile product was first discovered over 100 years ago, by the coloured population of the Cederberg area. They picked the wild Aspalathus linearis, known as rooibos ('red bush'), and bruised the leaves with hammers before drying them in the sun and making a refreshing tea-like drink.

In 1905 a Russian immigrant, Benjamin Ginsberg, began to exploit its potential, and by the 1930s Clanwilliam had become the centre of production. Today it is drunk throughout South Africa and exported around the world. It is low in tannin and free of caffeine, so very good for you. It is alleged to help those suffering from insomnia, indigestion, hay fever and even nappy rash (applied, cold, to the skin in this last case!). It can also be used for cooking, incorporated into soups, cakes, stews, and all manner of hot and cold drinks.

Visitors to Clanwilliam, a rural town in the shadow of the Cederberg Mountains, can tour the vast fields of rooibos and see the processing sheds on the area's Rooibos Route (www.rooibos-route.co.za). The town's Rooibos Teahouse (www.rooibosteahouse.co.za) also offers tastings. Rooibos recipes can be found at www.rooiboslitd.co.za.

Boerewors take-away

fiery Madagascan green pepper sauce. Fries are the most common accompaniment, though baked potatoes, sweet-potato chips, rice or salad may also be offered, together with a selection of vegetables. Steakhouse chains such as Spur (www.spur.co.za) are a good option for those on tighter budgets or travelling with children. Many restaurants offer low-carb dishes, catering to Banting (known locally as the Noakes diet).

The influence of German settlers can be seen in the range of spiced *boerewors* ('farmer's sausages') and dried *droewors* made by Afrikaans *slaghuis* (butchers). Jerky-like *biltong* is a South African speciality that evolved centuries ago, when meat could best be preserved by spicing, salting and drying. Beef biltong is the most common, but it is also made from game. It can be bought packaged in strips, and is increasingly to be found on restaurant menus, usually shaved over salad. Trying it is a must, but it is not to everyone's taste!

Breakfast Afrikaans-style is a hearty affair, often including many eggs, several rashers of bacon, boerewors and perhaps even some steak. Don't panic if you can't face such huge feasts; it is equally easy to start the day with muffins or fresh fruit.

Vegetarians need not despair. A huge selection of fresh salads and vegetables are available year-round, with most menus offering vegetarian options. If you can't locate a specialist vegetarian restaurant, Indian restaurants are well represented and always offer a great selection of meat-free dishes.

DESSERTS

Local delicacies include malva, made from cream, sugar and apricot conserve, and Cape brandy pudding, a steamed dessert soaked with brandy. Equally tasty, but less guilt-inducing, is the plentiful fresh fruit. If you don't have a sweet tooth, South African cheeses are very good, and you will usually be offered local versions of the European classics such as brie.

WHAT TO DRINK

South Africa is the world's eighth-largest wine producer, with over 600 wineries producing over 10 million hectolitres annually (over a billion bottles), which are considerably cheaper at source than overseas. The industry is concentrated almost exclusively in the Western Cape, spreading outwards from traditional centres such as Constantia, Stellenbosch, Franschhoek and Paarl into newer areas such as the Hemel en Aarde and Robertson valleys. You could spend weeks tasting on the wines estates, a pleasant activity incurring little or no charge and is often hosted by the winemaker or a knowledgeable sommelier.

The most common white grapes are Chenin Blanc, Columbard (used mainly for brandy), Chardonnay and Sauvignon Blanc, with varietals such as Viognier often appearing in blends. The leading red grapes are Cabernet Sauvignon, which tends to produce wines that are well suited to cellaring, Shiraz and Merlot. They are often blended, sometimes with Cabernet Franc in the mix, and Bordeaux blends are common. For something different, try a Pinotage, a robust, fruit-forward red that is unique to South Africa. Other varietals well known to international wine-lovers, for instance Pinot Noir and Semillon, are relatively poorly represented and most likely to appear in blends, though this is changing.

The Cape is so steeped in wine culture that it is common practice to bring your own wine to restaurants, and corkage is usually reasonably charged. Most restaurants have a good list of local wines at hugely marked-up prices.

Wine bar in Cape Town

Lager is also a popular choice, usually served very cold, and there is a lively microbrewery scene, documented by The Brewmistress (www.brewmistress.co.za). In Cape Town, try Mitchell's (www.mitchells-ale-house.com); at the V&A Waterfront, the Woodstock Brewery (www.woodstockbrewery.co.za); and Banana Jam (www.bananajamcafe.co.za) in Kenilworth, Southern Suburbs among many others. Among the commercial lagers, Namibia-made Windhoek (www.windhoekbeer.com) is a good choice. Drinkers with a sweet tooth will enjoy the Baileys-like Amarula Cream (www.amarula.com), made with marula fruit in Limpopo; it's mixed with coffee liqueur in the local Dom Pedro dessert cocktail.

For non-drinkers, there is a vast choice of fresh fruit juices, including apricot, guava and pear, and a burgeoning coffee scene, with buzzy coffee shops throughout Cape Town and chains such as Bootlegger (www.bootlegger.co.za) and Woolworths (www.woolworths.co.za) serving a good flat white.

PLACES TO EAT

Eating out in the Western Cape is a great pleasure, which can be enjoyed even on a budget. Dining in South Africa is relatively cheap by European standards and good value even for Americans. The standard of food is generally good, and the cosmopolitan nature of Cape Town means that visitors are spoilt for choice. Below is a selection of restaurants which offer good food, service and, in many cases, a delightful setting. There are lots more, so don't be afraid to look beyond these listings.

In general, staff in cafés and restaurants earn a pittance and are therefore dependent on tips to take home a good wage. A tip of 10 to 15 percent of the cost of the meal is the accepted norm. Service is mixed, and can be slow and inefficient in cafés and even restaurants, so only tip if you have enjoyed the experience.

The restaurants listed below are price-graded. These prices are based on the average cost of a three-course meal, excluding wine and tips:

$$$$$	over R500
$$$$	R400 to R500
$$$	R300 to R400
$$	R200 to R300
$	under R200

IN CAPE TOWN

95 Keerom $$$ *95 Keerom Street, Cape Town, tel: 021-422 0765,* www.95keerom.com. Dinner Monday–Saturday. This Italian restaurant, tucked away between Long Street and the Company's Garden, brings Milan to the Cape in dishes such as grilled black wildebeest, kudu and springbok with olive oil and rosemary. The Italian chef has previously won the World Pasta Championship. No children under 12.

Africa Café $$$ *108 Shortmarket Street, Heritage Square, tel: 021-422 0221,* www.africacafe.co.za. Dinner Monday–Saturday; lunch by arrangement. Excellent buffet of authentic African cuisine amid vibey decor, with a useful location near the Bo-Kaap in the city centre.

Aubergine $$$$$ *39 Barnet Street, Gardens, tel: 021-465 0000*, www. aubergine.co.za. Lunch Wednesday–Friday; dinner Monday–Saturday. Exquisite fusion dishes with lots of local influences and a good selection of vegetarian dishes. Wine-lovers should try the set dégustation menu, each course of which comes with a carefully selected Cape wine.

Bo-Kaap Kombuis $ *7 August Street, Bo-Kaap, tel: 021-422 5446*, www. bokaapkombuis.co.za. Lunch Tuesday–Sunday; dinner Tuesday–Saturday. With Table Mountain views, Bo-Kaap 'Kitchen' specialises in Cape Malay dishes from bobotie and bredie to curries and koeksister, in the area where this distinctive cuisine developed. Like most restaurants in this Islamic neighbourhood, it doesn't serve alcohol. Vegetarian options.

Bukhara $$$ *33 Church Street, city centre, tel: 021-424 0000*, www. bukhara.com. Lunch and dinner daily. Busy gourmet Indian restaurant with fine food, set menus and a drinks list stretching well beyond the usual Cobra Beer. Vegetarian options. Also at the V&A Waterfront.

Chef's Warehouse & Canteen $$$ *92 Bree Street, Heritage Square, tel: 021-422 0128*, www.chefswarehouse.co.za. Lunch and dinner Monday–Friday. Foodie tapas is all the rage in Cape Town, and there's no better place to try it than at Liam Tomlin's culinary wonderland, with its high-end kitchen products and basement bar. No reservations. It also has branches in Constantia and Franschhoek.

Den Anker Restaurant and Bar $$$ *Pierhead, V&A Waterfront, tel: 021-419 0249*. Lunch and dinner daily. This long-serving Waterfront favourite has a great open-air dining area, while the high-ceilinged interior is constructed around a ship-shaped bar. It serves Belgian specialities such as mussels and rabbit, and the wine list is supplemented by a range of imported Belgian beers.

Hokey Poke $ *1 Church Street, city centre, tel: 021-422 4382,* www.hokey-poke.co.za. Lunch and dinner Monday–Saturday. In a neon interior, enjoy a classic or build-your-own Hawaiian poke bowl. Choose a base, such as sticky rice or kale, a protein (tuna, salmon, beef, chicken, tofu) and add the toppings (edamame beans, pickled ginger, pickled beetroot, spring onions, friend macadamias) and sauce. Vegetarian options. Also in Sea Point and the V&A Food Market.

Jason Bakery $ *185 Bree Street, city centre, tel: 021-424 5644,* www.jasonbakery.co.za. Breakfast and lunch Monday–Saturday. The original Jason bakes the old-fashioned way, taking up to three days to produce its fresh breads. The hip Bree hangout does great breakfasts, such as avocado smash and poached egg on sourdough, and all-day eats from sandwiches to bacon-and-cheese croissants. Creations such as the doughnut-croissant 'doughsants' appeal to sweet teeth. Also in Green Point.

Lord Nelson Restaurant $$$$ *Mount Nelson Hotel, 76 Orange Street, Gardens, tel: 021-483 1000,* www.mountnelson.co.za. Dinner Monday–Saturday. South African food, such as ostrich carpaccio and springbok loin , in the grandest old hotel in Cape Town. Vegetarian options. There's also a bistro, Oasis, which hosts a Sunday jazz brunch in summer.

Mesopotamia $$ *36 Burg Street, tel: 021-424 4664,* www.mesopotamia.co.za. Lunch and dinner daily. At South Africa's original Kurdish restaurant, going since 1996, enjoy mezes and mains such as kebabs. There's tons of atmosphere, with hookah pipes, kilims on the floor and belly dancers to entertain.

La Parada $$ *Alfred Mall, V&A Waterfront, tel: 021-418 3003,* www.laparada.co.za. Breakfast, lunch and dinner daily. From its original branch on Bree Street, this homage to the Spanish good life has expanded to Constantia, Johannesburg and this Waterfront branch. Tapas from calamari to cauliflower popcorn are offered alongside mains. Vegetarian options.

Sevruga $$–$$$ *Quay 5, V&A Waterfront, tel: 021-421 5134,* www.sevruga.co.za. Lunch and dinner daily. The New York Times called this seafood restaurant 'the only reason to go to the V&A Waterfront', where it's well-positioned for watching the crowds drift past over a cocktail. After a few rounds of sushi and dim sum, you may share that critic's enthusiasm.

Signal Restaurant $$$$$ *West Quay Road, Cape Grace Hotel, V&A Waterfront,* tel: 021-410 7100, www.capegrace.com. Breakfast, lunch, tea and dinner daily. Elegant restaurant in five-star hotel, upstairs from Bascule whisky bar. Signal has a Cape Malay take on global cuisine with fresh seafood and vegetarian offerings as well. Tasting and pairing menus available.

OUTSIDE THE CITY CENTRE

Black Marlin $$ *Main Road, Miller's Point, Simon's Town,* tel: 021-786 1621, www.blackmarlin.co.za. Lunch and dinner daily. Seafood restaurant in an old whaling station. Good food and fine sea views, although it can get busy.

La Boheme Wine Bar and Bistro $$ *341 Main Road, Sea Point,* tel: 021-437 8797, www.labohemebistro.co.za. Lunch and dinner Monday–Saturday. This bistro offers great value two- and three-course dinner menus in an atmospheric setting. True to its European influences, it also does paella and tapas.

Codfather $$$$ *37 The Drive, Camps Bay,* tel: 021-438 0782, www.codfather.co.za. Lunch and dinner daily. A fun place that's always busy, with diners jostling for space at the seafood counters while the sushi belt goes round. Views of Lion's Head and knowledgeable waiters add to the experience.

La Colombe $$$$$ *Silvermist Estate, Constantia Nek,* tel: 021-794 2390, www.lacolombe.coza. Lunch and dinner daily. Run by a veteran of Gordon Ramsay's kitchen, this long-running favourite serves wonderful French and Asian fusion cuisine, accompanied by an optional wine pairing, on an elegant Constantia estate.

Greenhouse Restaurant $$$$$ *The Cellars Hohenort Hotel, 93 Brommersvlei Road, Constantia,* tel: 021-794 2137, www.greenhouserestaurant.co.za. Lunch Friday and Saturday; dinner Tuesday–Saturday. This is one of the grandest hotels in the Southern Suburbs, occupying an old mansion set in a magnificent garden in the heart of Constantia. Chef Peter Tempelhoff create gastronomic tasting menus, featuring dishes such as caramel smoked duck with truffled liver mousse, hibiscus beets and hazelnut and nasturtium crumble.

Jonkershuis $$$ *Groot Constantia, Constantia, tel: 021-794 6255,* www. jonkershuisconstantia.co.za. Breakfast and lunch daily; dinner Friday and Saturday. A little bit of everything, with an emphasis on classic Cape dishes such as Karoo lamb, in the delightful setting of the Cape's oldest wine estate. Only estate wines. Vegetarian options.

Two Oceans Restaurant $$$ *Cape of Good Hope Nature Reserve, tel: 021-780 9200,* www.two-oceans.co.za. Lunch and dinner daily. This large restaurant at Cape Point is a popular lunch stop thanks to its location, which offers staggering views back across False Bay. It serves a decent selection of seafood and other dishes, and has a lengthy wine list.

EXCURSIONS

Stellenbosch and the Winelands

Boschendal Deli$$ *R310, tel: 021-870 4213,* www.boschendal.com. Breakfast and lunch daily; dinner Saturday–Tuesday. This 17th-century wine estate's deli, on the Stellenbosch side of Franschhoek, offers country Cape cuisine in elegant Cape Dutch surroundings. Gourmet picnics are also available.

Bosman's $$$$$ *Grande Roche Hotel, Plantasie Street, Paarl, tel: 021-863 5100,* www.granderoche.com. Lunch and dinner daily. Run by a Michelin-trained executive chef, this Relais Gourmand restaurant offers top-class international cuisine, with the sommelier offering recommendations from the huge wine list to cater for every taste.

Marigold $$–$$$ *Heritage Square, 9 Huguenot Road, Franschhoek, tel: 021-876 8970*, www.marigoldfranschhoek.com. Lunch and dinner daily. North Indian cuisine may seem an unlikely choice in French-accented Franschhoek, but Marigold is under the same ownership as many of the town's finest establishments, and serves tandoori favourites in a contemporary dining room. Vegetarian options.

Reuben's $$$$ *2 Daniel Hugo Street, Franschhoek, 021-876 3772*, www.reubens.co.za. Lunch and dinner daily. On a quiet side street, local celebrity chef Rueben Riffel stirs up one of the best menus in Franschhoek, featuring mains from peppered springbok steak to parmesan gnocchi.

Stables $$–$$$ *Vergelegen Wine Estate, Somerset West, tel: 021-847 2156*, www.vergelegen.co.za. Breakfast and lunch daily. Casual and contemporary, this restaurant on the historic Vergelegen estate has an excellent bistro menu and a playground nearby, managing to please pretty much everybody.

Wijnhuis $$$ Corner of Church and *Andringa Streets, Stellenbosch, tel: 021-887 5844*, www.wijnhuis.co.za. Lunch and dinner daily. This wine bar and grill makes for a great introduction to the wines of Stellenbosch. The wine list includes over 500 selections, with 20 available by the glass or as a tasting, and the menu ranges from sandwiches to steaks.

Hermanus and the tip of Africa

Bientang's Cave $$$ *Beachfront, Hermanus, tel: 028-312 3454*, www.bientangscave.com. Lunch daily; dinner Friday and Saturday. Seafood served in a cave open to the ocean, reputed to have once been the home of a strandloper woman. Eat inside or out; either way, the location is spectacular, offering the chance to whale-watch as you enjoy fine food. Dinner hours vary, and it is best to call and check. Licensed.

Mogg's Country Cookhouse $$$ *R320, Hermanus, tel: 076 314 0671*, www.moggscookhouse.co.za. Lunch Wednesday–Sunday. At the end of a gravel road, just off the main Hemel en Aarde Valley road, you will re-

ceive a warm welcome at Mogg's. Simple farmhouse decor with a rustic but contemporary menu.

The Garden Route

101 Meade $$$ *101 Meade Street, George, tel: 044-874 0343,* www.101meade.co.za. Breakfast, lunch and dinner daily. The Garden Route's main town may not be its loveliest, but you'll be glad you stopped by this sophisticated bar-restaurant, which serves excellent food from breakfast to dinner.

34° South $$ *Knysna Quays, tel: 044-382 7331.* Breakfast, lunch and dinner daily. A well-established deli in the fabulous Knysna Quays serving everything from smoothies and soups to linefish and oysters.

West Coast

Die Strandloper $$$ *On the beach, Langebaan, tel: 022-772 2490,* www.strandloper.com. Lunch Friday–Sunday; dinner Friday. A not-to-be-missed experience. Ten-course meal including all the local seafood you can imagine. Eat as much or as little as you like. Swim or sunbathe between courses. Cash only.

Evita se Perron $$$ *Darling, tel: 022-492 2831.* www.evita.co.za. Lunch Sunday; dinner Saturday and Sunday. Classic Cape dishes with satirical names such as 'reconciliation bobotie' accompany the one-man show performed most weekends by Pieter-Dirk Uys, the legendary drag artist and socio-political comedian. Check website for show times and book ahead. The restaurant opens outside performance times too.

A–Z TRAVEL TIPS

A SUMMARY OF PRACTICAL INFORMATION

A Accommodation 118
Airport 119
B Budgeting For
Your Trip 119
C Camping 120
Car Hire 120
Climate 121
Clothing 122
Crime And Safety 122
Customs And Entry
Requirements 123
D Driving 124
E Electricity 125
Embassies and
Consulates 125
Emergencies 126
G Getting There 126
H Health And Medical
Care 127
Holidays 128

L Language 129
LGBTQ Travellers 129
M Maps 129
Media 129
Money 130
O Opening Hours 130
P Police 130
Post Offices 132
Public Transport 131
R Religion 132
T Telephones 133
Tickets 133
Time Zones 133
Tipping 134
Toilets 134
Tourist Information 134
W Websites 135
Weights and
Measures 135
Y Youth Hostels 135

A

ACCOMMODATION (see also Camping, Youth Hostels and Recommended Hotels on pages 120, 135 and 136)

Cape Town and its environs offer accommodation of all standards and prices, from simple backpackers' hostels to five-star luxury hotels. The Tourism Grading Council of South Africa (TGCSA; www.tourismgrading. co.za) operates a one- to five-star grading system for accommodation, but many fine B&Bs opt not to participate.

Advance booking is essential during peak season (November to Easter), particularly during the South African school summer holidays (early December to mid-January), when prices can rise by up to 50 percent. See Cape Town Tourism (see page 134) for more information. Throughout the Western Cape you will encounter extremely well-run small independent hotels. The area is also well endowed with fine guest houses and B&Bs. Guest House Accommodation of Southern Africa (GHASA) supplies information and has an online booking service www.ghasa.co.za. A great way to meet the locals and discover off-the-beaten-track places is to stay in self-catering cottages, which are available to rent by the sea or on farms, where they are known as farmstays. Check out www.safarinow.com and www.farmstay.co.za.

The V&A Waterfront area is an enjoyable place to stay in the city centre, although the location carries a price tag. The main hotels here are set slightly away from the busy nightlife spots, so they are not too noisy, and it is safe to stroll between the restaurants and bars after dark. The Southern Suburbs are an excellent source of quiet, comfortable hotels and guest houses in safe areas within easy striking distance of the city centre, while the Southern Peninsula and the Winelands also offer lovely options. The city's excellent accommodation standards continue throughout the province to the Garden Route, where you need to book months in advance to score a room during the Christmas break.

Accommodation is generally family-friendly, although some expensive hotels in Cape Town and around the Western Cape will not accept children aged under the age of 12.

AIRPORT

Cape Town International Airport (tel: 021-937 1200; www.airports.co.za) flanks the N2 highway 22km (13 miles) east of the city centre. It has a bureau de change, duty-free facilities, car rental offices, bag-wrap machines, cafés and shops; a VAT refund office, a post office and a taxi cooperative; and a Cape Town Tourism desk, which can help with accommodation.

The most affordable way to travel to/from the city centre is the safe and modern MyCiti Bus (www.myciti.org.za), which costs R100 and departs every half-hour. Some upmarket hotels operate shuttle services, and almost all hotels will arrange transfers to/from the airport in advance. Backpacker Bus (tel: 082-809 9185; www.backpackerbus.co.za) offers shuttles to Cape Town (one/two passengers R250/370) and Stellenbosch (R280/480), while Randy's Tours (tel: 021-706 0166; www.randystours.com) operates a pricier shuttle to the city centre, V&A Waterfront, Green Point, Sea Point and Camps Bay. Private taxis (tel: 083-652 0786) cost around R300; Uber can be a cheaper option.

The airport has an isolated location; the best option in the vicinity is Hotel Verde (www.verdehotels.com), part of Africa's greenest hotel group.

B

BUDGETING FOR YOUR TRIP

Favourable exchange rates mean that it is easy to enjoy high-quality accommodation and catering without spending a fortune.

Air fares. These vary hugely, according to the time of year. April and May are usually the cheapest times to fly, and December and January the most expensive. Round-trip flights from the UK or Europe cost about £600–1,000, and from Australia A$1,750–2,000. Package tours may reduce the costs.

Accommodation. A double room in a luxurious four- to five-star hotel will cost anywhere from R1,500 to several thousand in Cape Town's best establishments. A good two- to three-star hotel might charge R800–1,500 for a double (again, prices can be higher in Cape Town); B&Bs can offer better value and more character. Beware of 'per person sharing' prices: solo travellers may have to pay a single supplement or even pay the double rate.

Meals and drinks. An average three-course meal costs around R350, a bottle of wine in a restaurant from R100, and a cup of coffee R25.

Sightseeing. Many museums and galleries charge a nominal entry fee and a few offer free admission. National parks and reserves charge higher fees, and attractions such as the Table Mountain Cableway, Zeitz MOCAA and guided tours to Robben Island are relatively pricey.

Taxis. Metered taxis cost around R10 per kilometre. Uber generally works out cheaper.

C

CAMPING

There is a good network of campsites in the rural areas and national parks around Cape Town. Private resorts are much better than the municipal campsites, in terms of washing and cooking facilities and safety, while rough camping simply isn't safe. Private resorts often have shops, cafés, braais (barbecue stands) and a swimming pool. Campers can often pitch their tent on backpacker hostels' grounds and use their facilities for a fee. For more information and bookings, visit www.campsa.co.za.

CAR HIRE (see also Driving)

Though public transport in Cape Town is the best in South Africa, the story is not always the same outside the city. With so many magnificent destinations to travel to, a car is invaluable.

Cars can be rented from desks at the airport and rental offices in the city. There are many in Cape Town, including Avis (tel: 011-387 8431; www.avis.co.za), Budget (tel: 011-387 8002; www.budget.co.za), Thrifty (tel: 010-494 3979; www.thrifty.co.za), Europcar (tel: 021-421

5190; www.europcar.co.za) and Hertz (tel: 021-935 4800; www.hertz.co.za). Local company Around About Cars (tel: 021-422 4022; www.aroundaboutcars.com) offers excellent deals and one-way rentals nationwide.

Car rental is not cheap, but rivalry between the big international names and smaller local organisations ensures that there are good deals to be had if you shop around. Local firms are generally cheaper, but if you decide to rent a car through one of the international names, you can pick it up in one city and deposit it in another.

Check that the rental includes collision damage and theft insurance, and breakdown and accident rescue, and be aware that some insurance does not include dirt roads. As in most countries, there is normally an excess, which you can reduce or waive for an extra fee, and the option of protecting tyres and windows for a daily charge.

If your driving licence isn't printed in English or doesn't bear your photograph, you will need an International Driving Permit to rent a car, which you must obtain before you arrive in South Africa. Most companies insist on the driver being aged at least 21, even 23; some levy a surcharge if the driver is younger or stipulate that your licence has been valid for a year or two.

Motorhome rental is big business in South Africa. Motorhome, 4WD and SUV rental companies with offices in the city include Britz (www.britz.co.za), Maui (www.maui.co.za), Kea Travel (www.keatravel.co.za) and Drive South Africa (www.drivesouthafrica.com).

CLIMATE

South Africa's seasons are the reverse of the northern hemisphere, with midwinter in June and July and high summer in December and January. It is generally a few degrees cooler by the coast than inland. Cape Town has a Mediterranean climate, with cool, wet winters and warm to hot, dry summers. Notwithstanding the drought experienced by Cape Town, late autumn (May) to early spring (September) is generally the wettest time, with short periods of heavy rain. Though the climate is temperate, it is liable to change suddenly, switching from bright sunshine to grey skies within minutes.

The chart below gives Cape Town's average minimum and maximum temperatures.

CLOTHING

Informal clothing is generally accepted everywhere, though good restaurants prefer smart casual dress, including closed shoes. A few posh places might require men to wear a collared shirt, or even a jacket and tie, particularly after 6pm. Always be prepared for the weather to change. Even in high summer, it is advisable to pack a jacket or sweater for sudden drops in temperature, or to wear on boat trips. Sandals, swimming costumes and sun hats are invaluable, as are comfortable shoes for hikes through forests, mountains and national parks.

CRIME AND SAFETY

The usual rules of self-preservation, which apply in any major city, should be followed with extra vigilance in Cape Town. The golden rule is to be sensible and be aware of what is happening around you.

Do not walk alone after dark, and never display expensive jewellery or cameras. If you think you are being followed, change direction or vary your pace and seek refuge in a public place. When returning to your hotel after dark, use the main entrance, and avoid unlit places.

	J	F	M	A	M	J	J	A	S	O	N	D
Max												
°C	26	27	26	23	20	18	17	18	19	21	24	25
°F	79	80	79	74	68	64	63	64	66	70	75	77
Min												
°C	16	16	15	13	11	9	8	9	10	12	14	15
°F	61	61	59	55	52	48	46	48	50	54	57	59

Use credit and debit cards, and keep the amount of cash you carry to a minimum. Watch out for groups of small children surrounding you, and don't carry valuables in easily accessible pockets. If the worst happens and you are mugged, remain calm and do not resist, as guns and knives are all too common.

When travelling by car after dark, be aware that car-jacking is on the increase in Cape Town. Again, there are obvious precautions to take: always keep doors locked and windows shut; plan your route in advance and make long journeys during daylight only; store personal items out of sight, and do so before arriving and parking; park only in well-lit areas; and never pick up hitchhikers.

Never venture into the Cape Flats townships unless on a guided tour – and even then, ensure that your tour guide is licensed and professional. Most crime is centred on areas tourists seldom visit, while areas such as the Garden Route and Little Karoo are extremely safe.

CUSTOMS AND ENTRY REQUIREMENTS

All visitors to South Africa need an undamaged passport valid for at least six months from your date of entry, with up to two blank pages available for the stamp. Citizens of most Commonwealth countries (excluding New Zealand), most Western European nations, Japan and the USA receive a free, 90-day visitor's permit on arrival. As regulations do change, it is a good idea to check with your travel agent, your country's online travel advisory, South African Home Affairs (www.dha.gov.za) or Brand South Africa (www.brandsouthafrica.com).

Children under the age of 18 require various extra documents to enter South Africa, including an unabridged birth certificate. If asked, you should be able to prove that you can support yourself while in the country. In practice, immigration officers rarely ask to see these documents.

Duty-free allowance. Travellers aged 18 and over are allowed to bring in 200 cigarettes, 250 grams of tobacco and 20 cigars; 1 litre of spirits and 2 litres of wine; 50ml of perfume and 250ml of toilet water; plus gifts and other souvenirs up to the value of R5000. Duty is levied at 20 percent over these allowances.

Currency. Importing and exporting rand is limited to R25,000 in notes, and you should technically declare foreign currency. Retain all currency-exchange receipts and paperwork in order to reconvert your unspent rand before you leave the country.

D

DRIVING (see also Crime And Safety)

Road conditions. With its excellent network of roads and light rural traffic, driving in South Africa can be very enjoyable. Watch out for animals, particularly at night in country areas, so heed the warning signs. It is also common to see labourers returning to the townships on foot alongside the highways; watch out for this, as they are often laden with bags and cannot move quickly out of the way.

Minibus taxis have an unwritten right of way, and they also frequently jump red lights. Their drivers often carry handguns, so it is not a good idea to object to their driving if you encounter one.

You will find overtaking drivers coming towards you, or driving up your rear bumper, in the assumption that you will move onto the hard shoulder to avoid an accident. Despite the threat of fines, you will also find that it is the norm in South Africa to drive way beyond the speed limit.

Rules and regulations. Foreign drivers' licences, printed in English and with a photograph, are valid in South Africa. Other drivers must obtain an International Driving Permit. You must have your licence with you at all times while driving. There are corrupt policemen, so if you are pulled over and fined, ask for a receipt or to pay at a police station.

South Africans drive on the left-hand side of the road, and speed limits are 60km/h (37mph) in built-up areas, 100km/h (60mph) on country roads and 120km/h (73mph) on major highways. Drivers and passengers are compelled by law to wear a seat belt.

In addition to roundabouts, you may encounter four-way stops. The person who gets to a stop sign first has right of way over drivers arriving at the other stops. At roundabouts and other junctions, give way to traffic coming from the right. Be aware that Capetonians tend to jump red lights.

Fuel costs. Compared to European prices, fuel is fairly cheap in Cape Town, though ongoing hikes have pushed petrol to around R17 (US$1.20) per litre. There are plenty of filling stations on the main roads, but far less when you venture off the beaten track. Many will be open 24 hours in urban areas, but opening hours can be much shorter in rural areas, so be sure to fill up when you get the opportunity.

Parking. There are a good number of car parks in Cape Town, and lots of parking meters and parking attendants. It is illegal to park on the opposite side of the road facing the oncoming traffic.

If you need help. If you are involved in an accident where no one is injured, you must inform the police and the rental company within 24 hours. If someone is hurt, you must not move the vehicles until the police have arrived. Swap names and insurance details with the driver of the other vehicle.

The Automobile Association of South Africa can be called upon for advice and emergency rescue (tel: 086-100 0234; www.aa.co.za).

Road signs. Road signs are generally in both English and Afrikaans. Occasionally they will only be in Afrikaans, so make sure you know the name of your destination in that language. Do not head off on any unsigned roads.

E

ELECTRICITY

The power supply is 220/230 volts at 50Hz. Most hotels have 110-volt sockets for electric razors. Take a three-point, round-pinned adaptor, though they are readily available to buy if you forget. Sockets for European-style plugs with two circular pins are also common.

EMBASSIES AND CONSULATES

Most embassies are in Pretoria, but many countries have consulates in Cape Town.

Australia: contact the high commission in Pretoria; 292 Orient Street; tel: 012-423 6000; www.southafrica.embassy.gov.au.

Canada: contact the high commission in Pretoria; 1103 Arcadia St; tel: 012-422 3000; www.canadainternational.gc.ca/southafrica-afriquedusud.

Ireland: 19th Floor, LG Building, 1 Thibault Square, Foreshore; tel: 021-419 0636/7; www.dfa.ie.

New Zealand: Eastry Road, Claremont; tel: 021-683 5762; www.nzembassy.com/south-africa.

UK: 15th Floor, Norton Rose House, 8 Riebeeck Street, Foreshore; tel: 021-405 2400; www.gov.uk/world/organisations.

US: 2 Reddam Ave, Westlake, Southern Suburbs; tel: 021702 7300; https://za.usembassy.gov.

EMERGENCIES

Ambulance: tel: **10177**

Netcare 911 medical emergencies (private service): tel: **082 911**

Police: tel: **10111**

Emergencies (from mobiles): tel: **112**

Cape Town 24-hour assistance: tel: **082 415 7127**

Cape Town emergencies (including fire service): tel: **107**

Cape Town emergencies (from mobiles): tel: **021-480 7700**

Cape Town Rape Crisis: tel: **021-447 9762**

Sea Rescue: tel: **112** or **021-434 4011**

Wilderness Search & Rescue: tel: **021-937 0300**

G

GETTING THERE

By air. There are an increasing number of direct flights to Cape Town International Airport from major European and US cities, including nonstop options from the likes of London. It may work out cheaper to travel via Johannesburg or the Middle East.

High season (November–March, but especially December, January and around Easter) is generally the most expensive time to travel, but there are fluctuations throughout the year.

Many tour operators offer package tours from North America, Europe or the UK. These tours can be all-inclusive, covering flights, accommodation, car hire or local transport, meals and excursions to areas such as the Garden Route and Winelands. They can represent significant savings on booking all elements individually, though you may find yourself tied in to a group itinerary. London-based specialist operators, such as Expert Africa (tel: +44 20 3405 6666; US Toll Free 800-242-2434; www.expertafrica.com) and Rainbow Tours (tel: +44 20 3131 5300; www.rainbowtours.co.uk), will tailor holidays for individuals with a less restricted budget, preparing itineraries to suit the specific interests of their clients.

Fly-drive deals are also available through many airlines in conjunction with international car rental companies.

By rail. Trains operate daily to Cape Town from other parts of South Africa, covering vast distances in journeys that can last up to 24 hours. A popular, if expensive, option is to travel to Cape Town from elsewhere in South Africa on one of the famous luxury trains, which offer an irresistible combination of lavish accommodation and glorious, ever-changing scenery. The best-known of these are the Blue Train and Rovos Rail, which travel between Cape Town and Pretoria.

By sea. As befits a destination with such a long association with seafarers, Cape Town is on the route for a number of cruise lines, and it is also possible to travel as a passenger on board a cargo ship.

HEALTH AND MEDICAL CARE

Cape Town has excellent medical services, and hotels can usually call a doctor for guests. Although patients are generally referred to a hospital by a doctor, in an emergency head straight for the casualty department of the nearest hospital. Outpatient treatment is available, but you should take out medical insurance before you travel.

Pharmacies. Consult Google or the Yellow Pages for the pharmacy closest to you. Not all pharmacies are open outside regular shopping hours, but those with extended opening hours include Hypermed Pharmacy, York Road and Main Road, Green Point (tel: 021-434 1414; www. alphasvr.co.za), open 8.30am–7pm Monday–Saturday, and 9am–7pm Sunday; and the 24-hour M-Kem on Durban Road next to the N1 highway (tel: 021-948 5706; www.mkem.co.za).

No inoculations are mandatory for travel to South Africa, unless you have come from a yellow fever zone, in which case immigration officials will likely ask to see a vaccination certificate. It is advisable to make sure that your routine travel vaccinations, including tetanus and polio, are current, as well as getting typhoid and hepatitis A inoculations. The greatest hazard to tourists is the African sun. Skin cancer is on the increase, so using a strong sunscreen and wearing a sun hat are essential. It is easy to burn as there is often a gentle breeze or cloud cover, so the scorching sun can feel deceptively cool. Rabies is present in the area, so assume the worst if you are bitten by an animal and go to hospital for treatment.

HOLIDAYS

1 January	New Year's Day
21 March	Human Rights Day
Good Friday	March/April
Family Day	(Easter Monday – March/April)
27 April	Freedom Day
1 May	Workers' Day
16 June	Youth Day
9 August	National Women's Day
24 September	Heritage Day
16 December	Day of Reconciliation
25 December	Christmas Day
26 December	Day of Goodwill

L

LANGUAGE

There are 11 official languages in South Africa, with the three most common in the Western Cape being Afrikaans, English and Xhosa. English is the language of administration and tourism, so almost everyone speaks it, at least to some degree. Afrikaans is closely related to Dutch. The 'g' is pronounced with a guttural 'kh', 'oe' is pronounced 'oo', 'v' is pronounced 'f', and 'w' is usually pronounced 'v'.

LGBTQ TRAVELLERS

As Africa's gay capital, Cape Town welcomes LGBTQ travellers. South Africa has a progressive, gay- and lesbian-friendly constitution, and became one of the first countries to legalize same-sex marriage in 2006. There are many LGBTQ bars, clubs and restaurants around De Waterkant and Green Point, and annual events including the Mother City Queer Project (www.mcqp. co.za) in December. Useful websites include www.gaycapetown4u.com, www.mambaonline.com, www.mambagirl.com and www.gaysaradio.co.za.

M

MAPS

Cape Town Tourism (see page 134) and regional tourist offices can provide good maps, usually free of charge. In addition, more detailed commercially produced maps, available at most bookshops, may be useful for those who plan to head off the main routes and explore the dirt roads. Slingsby Maps (www.slingsbymaps.com) are the best for off-roading and hiking.

MEDIA

Radio and television. The main state television channels, run by the South African Broadcasting Corporation (SABC; www.sabc.co.za), are SABC 1, 2 and 3. SABC 1 broadcasts almost entirely in English; the other two broadcast a mixture of several languages.

The English-language SAFM radio station (104–107FM; www.safm.co.za) provides good morning and evening news programmes.

Newspapers. Newspapers are published in English and Afrikaans. National English-language newspapers include the *Sowetan* (www.sowetanlive.co.za) and *Star* (www.iol.co.za/the-star) dailies, the *Sunday Times* (www.timeslive.co.za) and the Friday *Mail & Guardian* (www.mg.co.za). The *Cape Times* (www.iol.co.za/capetimes) and *Cape Argus* (www.iol.co.za/capeargus) are local English-language dailies.

MONEY

Currency. The South African currency, the rand, is divided into 100 cents. R200, R100, R50, R20 and R10 banknotes are issued.

Exchange facilities. Money can be changed at banks and bureaux de change at the airport, V&A Waterfront and throughout Cape Town. Some hotels also offer an exchange facility, but charge a high commission. Withdrawing cash from an ATM using your home credit or debit card is easier.

Credit cards. International credit and debit cards are widely accepted throughout the Western Cape, especially Visa and MasterCard, but also American Express and Diners Club.

O

OPENING HOURS

Banks typically open 9am–3.30pm Monday–Friday and 9am–11am Saturday, while bureaux de change generally keep longer hours.

Most shops open 8.30am–5pm Monday–Friday, and until 1pm on Saturday. Supermarkets and malls tend to close later, often opening all day Saturday and Sunday.

P

POLICE

In an emergency contact the Police Flying Squad (tel: 10111; www.saps.co.za).

Good morning	**Goeiemôre**
Good afternoon	**Goeiemiddag**
Good night	**Goeienag**
Goodbye	**Totsiens**
Please	**Asseblief**
Thank you	**Dankie**
How much...?	**Hoeveel...?**
What is the time?	**Hoe laat is dit?**
Where is...?	**Waar is...?**

Members of the South African Police are armed, and wear blue uniforms and peaked caps. The growing importance of tourism to South Africa is producing a more tourist-friendly police force, but their past role as enforcers of apartheid and more contemporary image as corrupt and uninterested in solving crime mean that they are not greatly respected by many citizens. There are corrupt policemen on the streets, so if you are fined, ask for a receipt or to pay at a police station. Around central Cape Town, you will see tourist police booths, run by the Central City Improvement District (CCID; tel: 082 415 7127; www.capetownccid.org).

POST OFFICES

There are post offices (www.postoffice.co.za) in locations including Loop Street, the V&A Waterfront and the airport. Smaller post offices close at lunchtime). Postboxes are painted red. A better option is PostNet (www.postnet.co.za), with branches including 55 Kloof Street, Gardens.

PUBLIC TRANSPORT

Unlike many other South African cities, Cape Town has reasonable public transport.

Buses. Safe and modern MyCiti (www.myciti.org.za) commuter buses travel around the city centre, to various locations. CitySightseeing

one	**een**	six	**ses**
two	**twee**	seven	**sewe**
three	**drie**	eight	**agt**
four	**vier**	nine	**nege**
five	**vyf**	ten	**tien**

(www.citysightseeing.co.za) offers various routes around the city and peninsula on its open-topped hop-on, hop-off buses.

A number of luxury intercity coach companies operate from Cape Town along the major tourist routes such as the Garden Route. These include Intercape (tel: 021-380 4400; www.intercape.co.za) and Greyhound (tel: 087-352 0352; www.greyhound.co.za). The backpacker-orientated Baz Bus (www.bazbus.com) and Mzansi Experience (www.mzansi.travel), run along the east coast between Cape Town and Durban via the Garden Route.
Railway. Trains run from the city centre through the suburbs to Simon's Town on the False Bay coast.
Taxis. Metered taxis are available from taxi ranks around the city, or can be ordered by phone. Local companies include Rikkis (www.rikkis.co.za), Excite (www.excitetaxis.co.za) and Sport (www.sport24hrs.co.za). Uber is often cheaper and faster. Shared minibus taxis are not recommended for tourists. They can be hailed from the street, but are usually driven recklessly.

R

RELIGION
Although the majority of South Africans are Christian, all denominations are represented, and Cape Town has many places of worship, including churches, mosques, temples and synagogues. The city has a sizeable (and generally moderate) Muslim community, focused on the Bo-Kaap neighbourhood.

T

TELEPHONES

The international dialling code for South Africa is +27. The dialling code for Cape Town is 021 from within South Africa; drop the 0 if calling from abroad. The international access code to dial out of South Africa is 00, followed by the relevant country code.

Mobile phones, operating on the GSM digital system, work well and are extremely common. Depending on how often you use your phone outside of the widespread wi-fi networks, and where you are most likely to call regularly, it may work out cheaper to buy a South African SIM card for the duration of your stay. The main providers are MTN (wegotu.mtn.co.za), Virgin Mobile (www.virginmobile.co.za), Cell C (www.cellc.co.za) and Vodacom (www.vodacom.co.za); SIM cards can be bought for about R20 (US$1.40) at any of their outlets, as well as at most large supermarket chains. You will have to 'RICA' (register) your SIM when you buy it, so take your passport and proof of local address (which can be an accommodation receipt, reservation or letter). Various prepaid airtime and data bundles are available.

TICKETS

Tickets for concerts, theatre, opera and ballet performances, children's entertainment and sports matches are bookable through Computicket (tel: 0861 915 8000; www.computicket.com), which has a booth at Victoria Wharf Shopping Centre at the V&A Waterfront.

TIME ZONES

Cape Town (and all of South Africa) is two hours ahead of Greenwich Mean Time, seven hours ahead of US Eastern Standard Time and one hour in advance of British Summer Time and Central European Time. There is no daylight-saving period.

TIPPING

Waiters and waitresses should receive 10–15 percent on top of the bill, unless a service charge is included already. You can round the fare up for taxi drivers, or tip 5–10 percent, and give about 10 percent to tour guides. R10–20 is appropriate for hotel porters, and R20 per week for hotel maids.

Tip car guards around R2 to R5 for longer stays. In addition, all petrol stations use attendants, who should be tipped R5 for filling your tank and cleaning your windows, or R10 if they check your oil and water or tyre pressure. Wages are low in South Africa, so tips are always appreciated.

TOILETS

Good public toilets can usually be found in shopping centres, petrol stations and tourist attractions. Facilities at national parks and beaches may be more basic, but the standard of hygiene is usually acceptable.

TOURIST INFORMATION (see also Websites)

Before your trip, contact the South African Tourism branch in your home country, or check www.southafrica.net. In addition to the following, there are offices in Frankfurt, Amsterdam, Mumbai, Sao Paulo and Lagos.

Australia: Suite 302, Level 3, 117 York Street, Sydney; tel: +61 2 9261 5000; email: info.au@southafrica.net.

UK: 2nd Floor, 1–2 Castle Lane, London SW1E 6DR; tel: +44 20 8971 9350; email: info.uk@southafrica.net.

A helpful first port of call in central Cape Town is Cape Town Tourism's head office in the Pinnacle Building, corner Burg and Castle streets; tel: 086 132 2223; www.capetown.travel. A good network of tourist information offices operates throughout the Western Cape province. Every region, however small, has its own tourist board, but many offices close over weekends. For information on the whole Western Cape, check www.goto.capetown, which lists all the regional tourist offices.

W

WEBSITES

It is possible to gather a vast amount of information before you travel. In addition to the websites listed under Tourist Information, useful and informative sites include:

www.brandsouthafrica.com News and practical information.
www.netwerk24.com/weg/go Local travel magazine.
www.gardenroute.org.za Garden Route tourism.
www.iziko.org.za Links to many of the museums in Cape Town.

WEIGHTS AND MEASURES

South Africa uses the metric system.

Y

YOUTH HOSTELS

There are many youth hostels and backpackers' lodges in and around Cape Town. Numerous websites give links to youth hostels and lodges, including www.hostels.com, www.hostelworld.com, www.travel-nownow.co.za and www.coastingafrica.com. There are hostels affiliated with Hostelling International (www.hihostels.com/destinations/za/hostels) in Cape Town, Swellendam and Wilderness.

Some of the most comfortable backpackers' digs in Cape Town include the following, which are all in the City Bowl: Ashanti Lodge, 11 Hof Street, Gardens, tel: 021-423 8721, www.ashanti.co.za; The Backpack, 74 New Church Street, Tamboerskloof, tel: 021-423 4530, www.backpackers.co.za; and Once in Cape Town, 73 Kloof Street, Gardens, tel: 087 057 2638, www.once.travel.

⬛ RECOMMENDED HOTELS

Cape Town has a wide range of accommodation, so whether you are looking for a hip hangout or a snug home-from-home with sea views, you will not be disappointed. Most of the big luxury hotels are located in the city centre, on the V&A Waterfront and along the Atlantic seaboard, and are relatively pricey – in line with international prices. Better options are the smaller boutique hotels and guest houses in the city centre, the City Bowl suburbs climbing Table Mountain, Constantia and the Southern Suburbs. If you want the most cosmopolitan experience, close to a range of restaurants and the popular beaches, find a place in the city centre, City Bowl or Atlantic seaboard. For more tranquility and affordability, head for the Southern Suburbs or Southern Peninsula.

The hotels below are price-graded and all take major credit cards. These prices are based on the average cost of a double room:

$$$$$	over R4,000
$$$$	R3,000 to R4,000
$$$	R2,000 to R3,000
$$	R1,000 to R2,000
$	under R1,000

IN CAPE TOWN

Breakwater Lodge $$$ *Portswood Road, V&A Waterfront, Cape Town 8001, tel: 021-406 1911, www.bwl.co.za*. This former prison is now a Marriott hotel with a superb location. The rooms are basic but comfortable. Business centre. Disabled access. 327 rooms.

The Cape Grace $$$$$ *West Quay Road, V&A Waterfront, Cape Town 8002, tel: 021-410 7100, www.capegrace.com*. Its prime location on the Waterfront, with wonderful views of Table Mountain and the Zeitz MOCAA, make this a much sought-after hotel at the luxury end of the market. Bascule Bar, one of the southern hemisphere's best-stocked whisky bars, and Signal Restaurant add to the appeal Swimming pool, library, boardroom. Disabled access. 102 rooms.

Cape Heritage Hotel $$$$ *90 Bree Street, Cape Town, tel: 021-424 4646*, www.capeheritage.co.za. Modern facilities in an 18th-century house in the heart of the city, close to Heritage Square and the Bo-Kaap. Ideal for exploring the city and for access to shops and restaurants. 17 rooms.

Daddy Long Legs $$ *134 Long Street, Cape Town, tel: 021-422 3074*, www.daddylonglegs.co.za. Cape Town's pioneering art hotel, Daddy Long Legs consists of a dozen artistically and eccentrically decorated rooms, each with a different theme. The hotel and nearby self-catering apartments are ideally located to explore the nightlife around Long and Bree Streets.

Four Rosmead Boutique Guesthouse $$$$ *4 Rosmead Road, Oranjezicht, tel: 021-480 3810*, www.fourrosmead.com. Situated in an upmarket mountainside neighbourhood, this stylish small hotel combines refurbished late Victorian architecture with understated decor featuring contemporary South African artworks, and superb views to Table Bay and Table Mountain. 10 rooms.

iKhaya Guest Lodge $$ *Dunkley Square, Gardens, Cape Town, tel: 021-461 8880*, www.ikhayalodge.co.za. Woodcarvings, shweshwe cushions and sandstone walls emphasise the African ambience of this small lodge in the heart of the historic city centre. 16 rooms, including some self-catering apartments.

Mount Nelson Hotel $$$$$ *76 Orange Street, Gardens 8000, tel: 021-483 1000*, www.mountnelson.co.za. This gracious landmark, known affectionately as 'the Nellie', is the symbol of elegance and the height of luxury, with Winston Churchill, John Lennon and Nelson Mandela among the previous guests. Afternoon tea on the terrace - with a view of the exquisitely tended gardens - is a Cape Town institution, while the chic Planet Bar features celestial décor and an impressive drinks menu. In 2018, Condé Nast Traveller named this Belmond hotel the best in Africa, the Middle East and the Indian Ocean. Spa, swimming pool, tennis, hair and beauty salon. Disabled access. 225 rooms.

Peninsula All-Suite Hotel $$$$ *313 Beach Road, Green Sea Point, tel: 021-430 7777*, www.peninsula.co.za. The spacious studios and apartments in this seafront tower block in Sea Point are particularly suited to long-stay visitors and families seeking to keep down costs by self-catering. Facilities include a gym, a 'tech room' full of games consoles and a swimming pool. 110 rooms.

Taj Cape Town $$$$$ *1 Wale Street, Cape Town 8001, tel: 021-819-2000*, www.tajhotels.com. With direct access to the pedestrianised thoroughfare of St. George's Mall, this 5-star Taj hotel is housed in the former building of the South African Reserve Bank. Excellent for business and leisure travellers alike, with an acclaimed Indian restaurant, Bombay Brasserie. Full service spa and fitness centre.

OUTSIDE THE CITY CENTRE

The Bay Hotel $$$$$ *69 Victoria Road, Camps Bay 8040, tel: 021-430 4444*, www.thebay.co.za. All rooms enjoy views of the Atlantic Ocean or the Twelve Apostles. The hotel overlooks the beach of this trendy resort just 10 minutes from central Cape Town. Swimming pools, spa, gym, bike rentals, tennis and squash courts. 78 rooms.

The Cellars Hohenort $$$$$ *93 Brommersvlei Road, Constantia 7800, tel: 021-794 2137*, www.thecellars-hohenorthotel.com. Sister hotel to The Plettenberg (Plettenberg Bay) and The Marine (Hermanus), this historic Cape Dutch hotel, set in beautiful landscaped gardens in the Constantia Valley, conveys the feel of old-world luxury with a decidedly tasteful modern twist. The Greenhouse restaurant here is one of Cape Town's best and most experimental. Two swimming pools, spa, tennis court, croquet and pétanque. Relais & Châteaux member. 51 rooms.

Chartfield Guesthouse $$ *30 Gatesville Road, Kalk Bay, tel: 021-788 3973*, www.chartfield.co.za. For a seaside stay in cultural Kalk Bay, head to this late 19th-century pile with its whimsical sculptures overlooking the swimming pool and whitewashed interiors. Accommodation ranges from loft rooms to self-catering apartments.

Ellerman House $$$$$ *180 Kloof Road, Bantry Bay 8005, tel: 021-430 3200*, www.ellerman.co.za. Located on the side of Lion's Head in beautiful Bantry Bay, with a clear view to the Atlantic, this Edwardian-mansion-turned-boutique-hotel houses a contemporary art gallery with works by some of South Africa's greatest talents, as well as a cluster of private villas (great for groups and families) and a stunning menu of African fusion cuisine. With a library, spa, gym, pool and wine collection, Ellerman is the ultimate in Cape Town luxury.

Hout Bay Hideaway $$$ *37 Skaife Street, Hout Bay, tel: 021-790 8040*, www.houtbay-hideaway.com. Blissfully secluded and exclusive, in gorgeous gardens just a few minutes from the beach and town centre. Its suites and apartment are all tastefully furnished, featuring spacious bedrooms, balconies and an eclectic mix of furniture, antique and modern. Swimming pool.

The Lord Nelson's Inn $$ *58 St George's Road, Simon's Town, tel: 021-786 1386*, www.lordnelsoninn.co.za. This delightful, small and long-serving inn has a nautical theme and colonial clocks. It offers unpretentious, homely and very reasonably priced accommodation, as well as various bars and lounges, all within walking distance of central Simon's Town and the museums.

Steenberg Hotel $$$$$ *Steenberg Estate, Steenberg Road, Constantia Valley 7945, tel: 021-713 2222*, www.steenbergfarm.com. This stunning wine estate dates back to 1682, with rooms in the old Cape Dutch manor house and the restored barn, some furnished with antiques. Catharina's offers exceptional South African cuisine, while Bistro Sixteen82 is a favourite for brunch and tapas. Swimming pool, golf, spa and winery. 24 rooms.

Twelve Apostles Hotel $$$$$ *Victoria Road, Oudekraal, tel: 021-437 9000*, www.12apostleshotel.com. Having survived a bush fire in 2007, this plush hotel offers incredible views of the Atlantic and breaching whales from its perch beneath the mountain range of the same name. It's out of town but a short drive from both Camps Bay and Llandudno, and its Leopard Bar serves a sumptuous afternoon tea. 70 rooms and suites.

EXCURSIONS
Stellenbosch and the Winelands

Grande Roche $$$$ *Plantasie Street, Paarl 7646, tel: 021-863 5100, www.granderoche.com.* Renowned for its famous Bosman's restaurant (see page 114), this luxury hotel is set among vineyards at the foot of Paarl Mountain. Amenities include gym, two swimming pools, tennis, massage, sauna and steam-room. 35 rooms.

Lanzerac Hotel & Spa Manor & Winery $$$$$ *1 Lanzerac Road, Stellenbosch 7600, tel: 021-887 1132, www.lanzerac.co.za.* One of the Cape's most gracious country hotels, set in its own 330-year-old wine estate, updated with a state-of-the art spa and indoor heated swimming pool, all in a quiet location at the start of the Jonkershoek Valley. Swimming pool, conference facilities. 53 rooms.

Oude Werf $$$$ *30 Church Street, Stellenbosch 7600, tel: 021-887 4608, www.oudewerf.co.za.* Friendly, helpful staff and good food at this delightfully historic inn, which offers modern rooms in South Africa's oldest hotel, in the heart of old Stellenbosch. Swimming pool. 58 rooms.

Le Quartier Français $$$$$ *corner of Wilhelmina and Berg Streets, Franschhoek, tel: 021-876 2151, www.lqf.co.za.* A boutique hideaway, set in beautiful and fragrant gardens and including La Petite Colombe, an outpost of Constantia's famous restaurant, alongside the gorgeous rooms, suites and three-bedroom villa. Swimming pool, complimentary minibar. 26 rooms.

Reeden Lodge $$ *Cabriere Street, Franschhoek, tel: 021-876 3174, www.reedenlodge.co.za.* Reeden's 10 cottages sleeping two to eight are scattered around an emerald lawn a short stroll from central Franschhoek. A great example of the delightful self-catering accommodation available in the Western Cape, it's situated on a peaceful farm with animals, a treehouse and plenty of space for children. Swimming pool.

Hermanus and the tip of Africa

Arniston Hotel $$$ *1 Main Road, Arniston, tel: 028-445 9000*, www.arnistonhotel.com. A modern hotel on the seafront of the beautiful Arniston Bay, a short walk from the tiny harbour and fishermen's cottages. Disabled access. Swimming pool. 30 rooms.

Auberge Burgundy $$$ *16 Harbour Road, Hermanus 7200, tel: 028-313 1201*, www.auberge.co.za. Luxury Provençal-style guest house in the centre of town. Beautiful courtyards and gardens. Swimming pool. 19 rooms.

The Marine $$$$$ *Main Road, Hermanus 7200, tel: 028-313 1000*, www.themarinehotel.co.za. Sister hotel to The Plettenberg (Plettenberg Bay) and The Cellars Hohenort (Constantia), this luxury hotel on the clifftop is perfect for whale-watching. Heated swimming pool and tidal pool. 42 rooms.

Whale Rock Lodge $$–$$$ *26 Springfield Avenue, Hermanus 7200, tel: 028-313 0014/5*, www.whalerock.co.za. Attractive thatched lodge, just a short walk from boat trips and whale-watching on the seafront. Swimming pool. 11 rooms.

The Garden Route

Belvidere Manor $$$$ *Lower Duthie Drive, Belvidere Estate, Knysna 6570, tel: 044-387 1055*, www.belvidere.co.za. Relaxing location overlooking Knysna Lagoon and the town. Reception and Caroline's Bistro are in the 19th-century Manor House, and there is a quaint pub with a yellowwood ceiling, the Bell Tavern. Guests stay in cottages, with verandas and fireplaces, in 10 hectares (25 acres) of gardens. Swimming pool. 28 cottages.

Bitou River Lodge $$–$$$ *R340, tel: 044-535 9577*, www.bitou.co.za. A luxurious owner-managed guest house consisting of just five rooms with private patios set along the forested banks of the Bitou River, about 10km (6 miles) from Plettenberg Bay.

Hunter's Country House $$$$$ *Off N2, tel: 044-501 1111*, http://countryhouse.hunterhotels.com. Luxury country house hotel between Knysna and

Plettenberg Bay, offering warm, personalised service of the highest quality. Swimming pool. Member of Relais & Châteaux. 27 rooms and garden suites.

Rosenhof Country House $$$$$ *264 Baron van Rheede Street, Oudtshoorn 6620, tel: 044-272 2232, www.rosenhof.co.za.* Delightful hotel with rooms opening onto a rose garden and views of the Swartberg Mountains. Good food served in dining room of main house, with a wine bar and picnics also available. 15 rooms.

Surfari $$ *Victoria Bay, tel: 044-889 0113, www.surfariresort.com.* In the coastal forest between George and Wilderness, this modern guest house offers double, family and dorm accommodation and sea views all the way to the horizon.

West Coast

Bushmanskloof Wilderness Reserve $$$$$ *R364, tel: 021-437 9278, www.bushmanskloof.co.za.* This thatched lodge north of Clanwilliam in the Cederberg Mountains offers the chance to immerse yourself in the beauty of this wild region, to view its incredible fynbos and wildlife such as Cape mountain zebras in their natural habitat, and to see some fine examples of Bushman rock art. Relais & Châteaux. Swimming pool.

Farmhouse Hotel $$ *5 Egret Street, Langebaan 7357, tel: 022-772 2062, www.thefarmhousehotel.com.* Comfortable accommodation in a mid-19th-century farmhouse close to the West Coast National Park, with views of the stunning Langebaan Lagoon. Swimming pool, restaurant. 22 rooms.

Kagga Kamma $$$$$ *Op die Berg, tel: 021-872 4343, www.kaggakamma.co.za.* Off the R303 between Ceres and Citrusdal, this private reserve has craggy scenery, rock art dating back 6,000 years, and activities including stargazing, nature drives and mountain biking. The idiosyncratic accommodation includes 'cave suites' and open-air 'rooms' on private platforms. Bar-restaurant, two swimming pools, campsites.

INDEX

Adderley Street 30
African penguins 58
Agulhas Lighthouse 69
Arniston 70

Babylonstoren 65
Baxter Theatre Complex 49
Bird Island 81
Bloubergstrand 80
Bo-Kaap 35
Boschendal 67
Boulders Beach 58
Buitenverwachting 47
Butterfly World 66

Cableway 41
Cango Ostrich Farm 75
Cape Agulhas 69
Cape Flats 50
Cape of Good Hope 57
Cape Point 57
Castle of Good Hope 27
Cederberg Wilderness Area 81
Chapman's Peak Drive 56
City Hall 29
Clanwilliam 83
Clifton 55
Constantia 46

Darling 80
De Hoop Nature Reserve 71
Delaire Graff 67
Delville Wood Memorial 34
De Tuynhuys 33
Devil's Peak 43
Die Braak 62
District Six 29

Dorp Street 62
Drakenstein Correctional Centre 65

Earth Fair Food Market 31
Evita se Perron 80

Fairview 66
Fish Hoek 58
Franschhoek 64

Garden Route National Park 73, 78
Goukamma Nature Reserve 74
Government Avenue 33
Green Point Lighthouse 55
Groot Constantia 46
Groote Kerk 30
Groote Post 80
Gugulethu 53

Harold Porter National Botanical Garden 68
Hermanus 66
Houses of Parliament 33
Hout Bay 56

Imizamo Yethu 53

Jager's Walk 58
Josephine Mill 50

Khayelitsha 53
Kirstenbosch National Botanical Garden 44
Klein Constantia 47
Knysna 75
Kommetjie 57

Kopanong 53
KWV 65

Lambert's Bay 81
La Motte 67
Langa 53
Langebaan Lagoon 80
Lion's Head 43
Llandudno 56
Long Street 32
Lutheran Church 32

Maltese Cross 82
Maritime Centre 38
Martin Melck House 33
Masiphumelele 53
Maynardville Open-Air Theatre 50
Mossel Bay 72
Muizenberg 59

Newlands Cricket and Rugby Stadium 49
Nobel Square 38
Noordhoek 57

Oom Samie Se Winkel 62
Oude Werf 61
Oudtshoorn 74

Paarl 65
Paternoster 81
Planetarium 34
Plettenberg Bay 77

Ramonza 73
Robben Island 50

Safari Ostrich Farm 83
Sandy Bay 56
Signal Hill 43

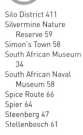
Silo District 411
Silvermine Nature
    Reserve 59
Simon's Town 58
South African Museum
    34
South African Naval
    Museum 58
Spice Route 66
Spier 64
Steenberg 47
Stellenbosch 61

St George's Cathedral 31
Stoney Point Nature
    Reserve 68
Storms River Mouth 79

Taal Monument 65
Table Mountain 40
Time Ball Tower 39
Tokora 67
Trafalgar Place Flower
    Market 30
Twelve Apostles 43

University of Cape
    Town 49

Vergelegen 68
Victoria and Alfred (V&A)
    Waterfront 37

Watershed 38
West Coast National
    Park 80
whales 70
Wilderness 73

INSIGHT GUIDES POCKET GUIDE

CAPE TOWN

First Edition 2019

Editor: Aimee White
Author: James Bainbridge
Head of DTP and Pre-Press: Rebeka Davies
Managing Editor: Carine Tracanelli
Picture Editor: Tom Smyth
Cartography Update: Carte
Photography Credits: Alamy 1; **Alex
Havret/Apa Publications** 4TL, 5MC, 5MC,
7R, 11, 15, 51, 75, 84, 99, 109; **Ariadne Van
Zandbergen/Apa Publications** 4MC, 4TC,
5T, 5M, 6L, 6R, 12, 30, 37, 49, 61, 62, 64, 66,
69, 72, 76, 78, 81, 87, 88, 96, 107; **Cape Town
Tourism** 4ML, 6/7, 26, 28, 42/43, 45, 52, 56,
59, 90, 92, 103, 104/105; **Getty Images** 16,
21, 22; **iStock** 5TC, 4/5M, 40, 82; **Public
domain** 19; **Shutterstock** 33, 34, 38, 47,
54, 71, 94
Cover Picture: Shutterstock

Distribution
UK, Ireland and Europe: Apa Publications
(UK) Ltd; sales@insightguides.com
United States and Canada: Ingram
Publisher Services; ips@ingramcontent.com
Australia and New Zealand: Woodslane;
info@woodslane.com.au
Southeast Asia: Apa Publications (SN) Pte;
singaporeoffice@insightguides.com
Worldwide: Apa Publications (UK) Ltd;
sales@insightguides.com

**Special Sales, Content Licensing
and CoPublishing**
Insight Guides can be purchased in bulk
quantities at discounted prices. We can
create special editions, personalised jackets
and corporate imprints tailored to your
needs. sales@insightguides.com;
www.insightguides.biz
All Rights Reserved
© 2019 Apa Digital (CH) AG and
Apa Publications (UK) Ltd
Printed in China by CTPS
No part of this book may be reproduced,
stored in a retrieval system or transmitted in
any form or means electronic, mechanical,
photocopying, recording or otherwise,
without prior written permission from Apa
Publications.

Contact us
Every effort has been made to provide
accurate information in this publication,
but changes are inevitable. The publisher
cannot be responsible for any resulting loss,
inconvenience or injury. We would appreciate
it if readers would call our attention to any
errors or outdated information. We also
welcome your suggestions; please contact
us at: hello@insightguides.com
www.insightguides.com